AF566849

FAO ANIMAL PRODUCTION AND HEALTH
manual

# SMALL-SCALE POULTRY PRODUCTION

technical guide

**E.B. Sonaiya**
Department of Animal Science
Obafemi Awolowo University
Ile-Ife, Nigeria
and
**S.E.J. Swan**
Village Poultry Consultant
Waimana, New Zealand

**2007**
**Published by Arrangement with the**
**Food and Agriculture Organization of the United Nations**
***by***
**DAYA PUBLISHING HOUSE**
**Delhi - 110 035**
**for Sale and Distribution only in South-East Asia**

First Indian Edition 2007

ISBN 81-7035-502-8

*Published by* : **Daya Publishing House**
1123/74, Deva Ram Park
Tri Nagar, Delhi - 110 035
Phone: 27383999
Fax: (011) 23244987
e-mail : dayabooks@vsnl.com
website : www.dayabooks.com

*Showroom* : 4760-61/23, Ansari Road, Darya Ganj,
New Delhi - 110 002
Phone: 23245578, 23244987

*Printed at* : **Salasar Imaging Systems**
Delhi - 110 35

PRINTED IN INDIA

# Foreword

Keeping poultry makes a substantial contribution to household food security throughout the developing world. It helps diversify incomes and provides quality food, energy, fertilizer and a renewable asset in over 80 percent of rural households.

Small-scale producers are however constrained by poor access to markets, goods and services; they have weak institutions and lack skills, knowledge and appropriate technologies. The result is that both production and productivity remain well below potential and losses and wastage can be high. However, adapted breeds, local feed resources and appropriate vaccines are available, along with proven technologies that can substantially improve productivity and income generation.

FAO recognizes the important contribution that poultry can make to poverty alleviation and has programmes that focus on small-scale, low-input, family based poultry production. These programmes target the more vulnerable households especially those affected by natural disasters, HIV Aids and conflict. This manual provides a comprehensive and valuable technical guide for those in government service or aid agencies, wishing to embark on projects that exploit the potential of small-scale poultry production to improve the livelihoods of the rural poor. All aspects of small-scale poultry production are discussed in this book including feeding and nutrition, housing, general husbandry and flock health. Regional differences in production practices are described.

FAO acknowledges and commends the effort that the authors have put into making such a comprehensive and valuable reference for those involved in poultry production in the developing world. The views expressed are, however, those of the authors and do not necessarily reflect those of FAO. Members of the International Network for Family Poultry Development (INFPD) have been involved in producing and reviewing this document and their contribution is also gratefully acknowledged. A major aim of the INFPD is to bring together and disseminate technical information that supports small-scale poultry producers throughout the world.

# Chapter 1
# Introduction

## The socio-economic Importance of Family Poultry

Family poultry is defined as small-scale poultry keeping by households using family labour and, wherever possible, locally available feed resources. The poultry may range freely in the household compound and find much of their own food, getting supplementary amounts from the householder. Participants at a 1989 workshop in Ile-Ife, Nigeria, defined rural poultry as a flock of less than 100 birds, of unimproved or improved breed, raised in either extensive or intensive farming systems. Labour is not salaried, but drawn from the family household (Sonaiya 1990b). Family poultry was additionally clarified as "small flocks managed by individual farm families in order to obtain food security, income and gainful employment for women and children" (Branckaert, as cited in Sonaiya, 1990c). Family poultry is quite distinct from medium to large-scale commercial poultry farming.

Family poultry is rarely the sole means of livelihood for the family but is one of a number of integrated and complementary farming activities contributing to the overall well-being of the household. Poultry provide a major income-generating activity from the sale of birds and eggs. Occasional consumption provides a valuable source of protein in the diet. Poultry also play an important socio-cultural role in many societies. Poultry keeping uses family labour, and women (who often own as well as look after the family flock) are major beneficiaries. Women often have an important role in the development of family poultry production as extension workers and in vaccination programmes.

For smallholder farmers in developing countries (especially in low income, food-deficient countries [LIFDC]), family poultry represents one of the few opportunities for saving, investment and security against risk. In some of these countries, family poultry accounts for approximately 90 percent of the total poultry production (Branckaert, 1999). In Bangladesh for example, family poultry represents more than 80 percent of the total poultry production, and 90 percent of the 18 million rural households keep poultry. Landless families in Bangladesh form 20 percent of the population (Fattah, 1999, citing the Bangladesh Bureau of Statistics, 1998) and they keep between five and seven chickens per household. In LIFDC countries, family poultry-produced meat and eggs are estimated to contribute 20 to 30 percent of the total animal protein supply (Alam, 1997, and Branckaert, 1999), taking second place to milk products (38 percent), which are mostly imported. Similarly, in Nigeria, family poultry represents approximately 94 percent of total poultry keeping, and accounts for nearly four percent of the total estimated value of the livestock resources in the country. Family poultry represents 83 percent of the estimated 82 million adult chickens in Nigeria. In Ethiopia, rural poultry accounts for 99 percent of the national total production of poultry meat and eggs (Tadelle *et al.*, 2000).

Poultry are the smallest livestock investment a village household can make. Yet the poverty-stricken farmer needs credit assistance even to manage this first investment step on the ladder out of poverty. Poultry keeping is traditionally the role of women in many developing countries. Female-headed households represent 20 to 30 percent of all rural households in Bangladesh (Saleque, 1999), and women are more disadvantaged in terms of options for income generation. In sub-Saharan Africa, 85 percent of all households keep poultry, with women owning 70 percent of the poultry. (Guéye, 1998 and Branckaert, 1999, citing World Poultry 14).

Income generation is the primary goal of family poultry keeping. Eggs can provide a regular, albeit small, income while the sale of live birds provides a more flexible source of cash as required. For example, in the Dominican Republic, family poultry contributes 13 percent of the income from animal production (Rauen *et al.*, 1990). The importance of poultry to rural households is illustrated by the example below from the United Republic of Tanzania (see Table 1.1). Assuming an indigenous hen lays 30 eggs per year, of which 50 percent are consumed and the remainder have a hatchability of 80 percent, then each hen will produce 12 chicks per year.

Assuming six survive to maturity (with 50 percent mortality), and assuming that three pullets and three are cockerels, the output from one hen projected over five years would total 120 kg of meat and 195 (6.8 kg) eggs.

**Table 1.1** Projected output from a single initial hen (United Republic of Tanzania)

| Time (months) | N° of hatching eggs | N° of cockerels | N° of pullets | N° of cocks | N° of hens | N° of culls |
|---|---|---|---|---|---|---|
| 0 | | | 1 | | - | |
| 8 | | | - | - | 1 | |
| 20 | 15 | 3 | 3 | - | - | 1 |
| 28 | - | - | - | 3 | 3 | - |
| 40 | 45 | 9 | 9 | - | - | 6 |
| 48 | - | - | - | 9 | 9 | |
| 60 | 135 | 27 | 27 | - | - | 18 |
| Total | 195 | 39 | 40 | 12 | 13 | 25 |

Source: Kabatange and Katule, 1989.

A study on income generation in transmigrant farming systems in East Kalimantan, Indonesia (see Table 1.2), showed that family poultry accounted for about 53 percent of the total income, and was used for food, school fees and unexpected expenses such as medicines (Ramm *et al.*, 1984).

Flock composition is heavily biased towards chickens in Africa and South Asia, with more ducks in East Asia and South America. Flock size ranges from 5 – 100 in Africa, 10 – 30 in South America and 5 – 20 in Asia. Flock size is related to the poultry farming objectives of:

- home consumption only;
- home consumption and cultural reasons;
- income and home consumption; and
- income only.

(See Table 1.3.)

In Bangladesh (Jensen, 1999), the average production rate per local hen of 50 eggs/year was regarded by some as low productivity. However, if it is considered that 50 eggs per hen per year represents four hatches from four clutches of eggs laid, incubated and hatched by the mother hen, and the outcome is 30 saleable chicken reared per year (assuming no eggs sold or eaten, 80 percent hatchability and 25 percent rearing mortality), then it is a remarkably high productivity.

## PRODUCTION SYSTEMS

Family poultry are kept under a wide range of conditions, which can be classified into one of four broad production systems (Bessei, 1987):

- free-range extensive;
- backyard extensive;
- semi-intensive; and
- intensive.

Indicative production levels for the different systems are summarized in Table 1.4.

**Table 1.2** Annual budget for a family farm with 0.4 ha irrigated paddy, 0.1 ha vegetable garden, 100 ducks and two buffaloes in Indonesia

| | Unit | Rupees |
|---|---|---|
| **Annual expenses** | | |
| Crops | | 1 198 000 |
| Animals: | | |
| - Buffaloes | | |
| - Ducks | | 1 147 200 |
| Subtotal | | 2 345 200 |
| **Annual revenue** | | |
| Crops: | | |
| - Maize | 240 kg | 96 000 |
| - Rice | 4 000 kg | 2 000 000 |
| - Cassava | 600 kg | 60 000 |
| - Peanut | 60 kg | 60 000 |
| - Soybean | 60 kg | 30 000 |
| - Mixed garden | | 150 000 |
| Subtotal Crops | | 2 396 000 |
| Animals: | | |
| - Buffaloes - meat | 150 kg | 300 000 |
| - draft | 30 days | 180 000 |
| Subtotal Buffaloes | | 480 000 |
| - Ducks - eggs | 13 140 eggs | 5 256 000 |
| Subtotal Animals | | 5 736 000 |
| **Annual net return to family labour from crops** | | 1 198 000 (20.7%) |
| **Annual net return to family labour from livestock** | | |
| - Buffaloes | | 480 000 (8.3%) |
| - Ducks | | 4 108 800 (71.0%) |
| **Total return to family labour from agriculture** | | 5 786 800 (100%) |

Source: Setioko, 1997.

**Table 1.3** Flock size and poultry farming objectives in Nigeria

| **Objectives** | **Flock size** | **% of sample** |
|---|---|---|
| Home consumption only | 1-10 | 30 |
| Home consumption and cultural reasons | 1-10 | |
| Income and home consumption | 11-30 | 44 |
| Income only | >50 | 10.5 |

Source: Sonaiya, 1990a.

**Free-Range Extensive Systems**

In Africa, Asia and Latin America, 80 percent of farmers keep poultry in the first two extensive systems. Under free-range conditions, the birds are not confined and can scavenge for food over a wide area. Rudimentary shelters may be provided, and these may or may not be used. The birds may roost outside, usually in trees, and nest in the bush. The flock contains birds of different species and varying ages.

**Backyard Extensive Systems**

Poultry are housed at night but allowed free-range during the day. They are usually fed a handful of grain in the morning and evening to supplement scavenging.

**Semi-Intensive Systems**

These are a combination of the extensive and intensive systems where birds are confined to a certain area with access to shelter. They are commonly found in urban and peri-urban as well as rural situations. In the "**run**" system, the birds are confined in an enclosed area outside during the day and housed at night. Feed and water are available in the house to avoid wastage by rain, wind and wild animals.

In the European system of free-range poultry keeping, there are two other types of housing. The first of these is the "**ark**" system, where the poultry are confined overnight (for security against predators) in a building mounted on two rails or skids (usually wooden), which enable it to be moved from place to place with draught power. A typical size is 2 × 2.5 m to hold about 40 birds.

The second type of housing is the "**fold**" unit, with a space allowance (stock density) for adult birds of typically 3 to 4 birds per square metre (birds/m$^2$), both inside and (at least this) outside. The fold unit is usually small enough to be moved by one person. Neither of these two systems is commonly found in developing countries.

**Intensive Systems**

These systems are used by medium to large-scale commercial enterprises, and are also used at the household level. Birds are fully confined either in houses or cages. Capital outlay is higher and the birds are totally dependent on their owners for all their requirements; production however is higher. There are three types of intensive systems:

- **Deep litter system**: birds are fully confined (with floor space allowance of 3 to 4 birds/m$^2$ within a house, but can move around freely. The floor is covered with a **deep litter** (a 5 to 10 cm deep layer) of grain husks (maize or rice), straw, wood shavings or a similarly absorbent (but non-toxic) material. The fully enclosed system protects the birds from thieves and predators and is suitable for specially selected commercial breeds of egg or meat-producing poultry (layers, breeder flocks and broilers).
- **Slatted floor system**: wire or wooden slatted floors are used instead of deep litter, which allow stocking rates to be increased to five birds/m$^2$ of floor space. Birds have reduced contact with faeces and are allowed some freedom of movement.
- **Battery cage system**: this is usually used for laying birds, which are kept throughout their productive life in cages. There is a high initial capital investment, and the system is mostly confined to large-scale commercial egg layer operations.

Intensive systems of rearing indigenous chickens commercially is uncommon, a notable rare exception being in Malaysia, where the industry developed in response to the heavy demand for indigenous chickens in urban areas (Supramaniam, 1988). However, this accounts for only two in every 100 000 (0.002 percent) of that country's indigenous chicken.

**Table 1.4** Production and reproduction per hen per year under the different management systems

| Production system | N° of eggs per hen/year | N° of year-old chickens | N° of eggs for consumption and sale |
|---|---|---|---|
| **Scavenging** (free-range) | 20-30 | 2-3 | 0 |
| **Improved scavenging**[1/] | 40-60 | 4-8 | 10-20 |
| **Semi-intensive** | 100 | 10-12 | 30-50 |
| **Intensive** (deep litter) | 160-180 | 25-30 | 50-60 |
| **Intensive** (cages) | 180-220 | - | 180-220 |

[1/] improved shelter and Newcastle Disease vaccination

Source: Bessei, 1987.

The above management systems frequently overlap. Thus free-range is sometimes coupled with feed supplementation, backyard with night confinement but without feeding, and poultry cages in confined spaces (Branckaert and Guèye, 1999).

## Conclusions

Over the last decade, the consumption of poultry products in developing countries has grown by 5.8 percent per annum, faster than that of human population growth, and has created a great increase in demand. Family poultry has the potential to satisfy at least part of this demand through increased productivity and reduced wastage and losses, yet still represent essentially low-input production systems. If production from family poultry is to remain sustainable, it must continue to emphasize the use of family labour, adapted breeds and better management of stock health and local feed resources. This does not exclude the introduction of appropriate new technologies, which need not be sophisticated. However, technologies involving substantially increased inputs, particularly if they are expensive (such as imported concentrate feeds or genetic material) should be avoided. This is not to say that such technologies do not have a place in the large-scale commercial sector, where their use is largely determined by economic considerations.

Development initiatives in the past have emphasized genetic improvement, usually through the introduction of exotic genes, arguing that improved feed would have no effect on indigenous birds of low genetic potential. There is a growing awareness of the need to balance the rate of genetic improvement with improvement in feed availability, health care and management. There is also an increased recognition of the potential of indigenous breeds and their role in converting locally available feed resources into sustainable production.

This manual aims to provide those involved with poultry development in developing countries with a practical guide and insight into the potential of family poultry to improve rural livelihoods and to meet the increasing demand for poultry products.

# Chapter 2
# Species and Breeds

## Different Poultry Species and Breeds

All species of poultry are used by rural smallholders throughout the world. The most important species in the tropics are: chickens, guinea fowl, ducks (including Muscovy ducks), pigeons, turkeys and geese. Local strains are used, but most species are not indigenous. The guinea fowl (*Numididae)* originated in West Africa; the Muscovy duck (*Cairina moschata*) in South America; pigeons *(Columba livea*) in Europe; turkeys *(Meleagrididae)* in Latin America; pheasants (*Phasianidae*) in Asia; the common duck *(Anas)* in Europe; and geese (*Anser*) in Asia.

Flock composition is determined by the objectives of the poultry enterprise (see Chapter 1). In Nigeria for example, the preference is for the smooth-feathered, multicoloured native chickens or Muscovy ducks. Multicoloured feathers serve as camouflage for scavenging birds against predators, including birds of prey, which can more easily see solid colours (especially white). Foundation stock is usually obtained from the market as grower pullets and young cockerels. A hen to cock ratio of about 5:1 is common. Both sexes are retained for 150 to 300 days, for the purposes of culling, selling, home consumption and gifts, most of which require adult birds.

In the last 50 years, there has been a great advance in the development of hybrid breeds for intensive commercial poultry production. This trend is most noticeable in chickens, turkeys and ducks. The new hybrids (those of chickens in particular) are widely distributed and are present in every country in the tropics, even in the most remote villages. The hybrids have been carefully selected and specialised solely for the production of either meat or eggs. These end-product-specialised hybrid strains are unsuitable for breeding purposes, especially for mixing with local village scavenger stock, as they have very low mothering ability and broodiness.

For the smallholder, keeping hybrids means considerable changes are required in management. These changes are expensive for the following reasons:

- All replacement day-old chicks must be purchased.
- Hatchery chicks require artificial brooding and special starting feed.
- Hybrids require higher quality balanced feed for optimum meat and egg production.
- Hybrids require more careful veterinary hygiene and disease management.
- Egg-laying hybrid hens require supplementary artificial light (a steadily increasing day-length up to 17 hours of total light per day) for optimum (profitable) egg production.

The meat and eggs from intensively raised hybrid stock are considered by many traditional consumers to have less flavour, and the meat to have too soft a texture. Consumers will thus often pay a higher price for village-produced poultry meat and eggs. Thus for rural family poultry keepers, it is more appropriate to maintain and improve local birds to meet this demand.

### Chickens

Chickens originated in Southeast Asia and were introduced to the rest of the world by sailors and traders. Nowadays, indigenous village chickens are the result of centuries of cross-breeding with exotic breeds and random breeding within the flock. As a result, it is not possible to standardize the characteristics and productive performance of indigenous chickens.

There is no comprehensive list of the breeds and varieties of chickens used by rural smallholders, but there is considerable information on some indigenous populations from various regions. Most of this is based on feather colour and other easily measured body features (genetic traits), but more detailed data are becoming available. Examples of local chickens from different parts of the tropics are given in Tables 2.1 to 2.3 below. These evaluations were usually carried out under intensive management conditions in research stations, as the objective was to evaluate the local birds' productivity. More recently, data on the performance of local chickens under extensive management have become available, which makes it possible to compare performance under extensive and intensive systems (see Table 2.3).

**Table 2.1** Performance of local breeds in South Asia (intensively housed)

| Traits | Desi | Naked Neck | Aseel | Kadak-anath | Black Bengal |
|---|---|---|---|---|---|
| 12 wk live wt (g) | 544 | 629 | 640 | NA | 433 |
| Age at 1st egg (d) | 208 | NA | 219 | NA | 200 |
| Eggs/hen/year | 116 | 104 | 100 | 80 | NA |
| Egg wt (g) | 46 | 45 | 51 | 39 | 49 |
| Fertility (%) | 81 | 80 | 55 | 90 | 86 |
| Hatchability (%) | 55 | 61 | 45 | 61 | 68 |

Source: Acharya and Kumar, 1984. *Desi* means "local" (as in Bangladeshi)

Characteristics such as adult body weight and egg weight vary considerably among indigenous chicken populations, although reproductive traits, such as the number of laying seasons per year, the number of eggs per clutch and hatchability are more consistent. *Desi* hens in Bangladesh range from 190 to 200 days of age at first egg (an easy measure of age-at-sexual-maturity), and they lay 10 to 15 eggs per season in 3 to 4 clutches (3 to 4 times) per year, with a hatchability of 84 to 87 percent (percent of eggs set) (Haque , 1999).

**Table 2.2** Local chicken breeds of Ethiopia

| Traits | Tukur | Melata | Kei | Gebsima | Netch |
|---|---|---|---|---|---|
| 24 wk body wt (g) | 960 | 1000 | 940 | 950 | 1180 |
| Age at 1st egg (d) | 173 | 204 | 166 | 230 | 217 |
| Eggs/bird.yr | 64 | 82 | 54 | 58 | 64 |
| Egg wt (g) | 44 | 49 | 45 | 44 | 47 |
| Fertility (%) | 56 | 60 | 57 | 53 | 56 |
| Hatchability (%) | 42 | 42 | 44 | 39 | 39 |

Source: Shanawany & Banerjee, 1991 as cited in Forssido, 1986; Australian Agricultural Consultancy and Management Company, 1984; Beker and Banerjee, 1990.

Indigenous village birds in Ethiopia attain sexual maturity at an average age of seven months (214 days). The hen lays about 36 eggs per year in three clutches of 12 to 13 eggs in about 16 days. If the hen incubates her eggs for three weeks and then rears the chicks for twelve weeks, then each reproductive cycle lasts for 17 weeks. Three cycles then make one year. These are very efficient, productive and essential traits for survival.

## Guinea fowl

Guinea fowl are native to West Africa but are now found in many parts of the tropics, and are kept in large numbers under intensive systems in France, Italy, the former Soviet Union and Hungary. In India, guinea fowl are raised in parts of the Punjab (Shingari *et al.,* 1994), Uttar Pradesh, Assam and Madhya Pradesh, usually in flocks of a few hundred birds. Guinea fowl are seasonal breeders, laying eggs only during the rainy season, under free-range conditions. They are very timid, roosting in trees at night, and although great walkers, they fly very little.

Guinea fowl thrive in both cool and hot conditions, and their potential to increase meat and particularly egg production in developing countries deserves better recognition. The first egg is normally laid at about 18 weeks of age, and unlike many indigenous birds (which produce a single clutch a year), guinea hens lay continuously until adverse weather sets in. In West Africa, laying is largely confined to the rainy season. Guinea hens under free-range conditions can lay up to 60 eggs per season, while well-managed birds under intensive management can lay up to 200 eggs per year. The guinea hen "goes broody" (sits on eggs in the nest) after laying, but this can be overcome by removing most of the eggs. A clutch of 15 to 20 eggs is common, and the incubation period for guinea fowl is 27 days. Domesticated guinea fowl under extensive or semi-intensive management in Nigeria were reported to lay 60 to 100 eggs with a fertility rate of 40 to 60 percent.

**Table 2.3** Performance of local chicken breeds under scavenging and intensive management systems

| System | Country | Breed | Body Wt (g) | Egg N° | Egg Wt (g) |
|---|---|---|---|---|---|
| **Scavenging** | | | | | |
| Africa | Burundi | Local | 1 500 | 75 | 40 |
| | Mali | Local | 1 170 | 35 | 34 |
| | United Rep.Tanzania | Local | 1 200 | 70 | 41 |
| Asia | Indonesia | Kampung | 2 000 | 35 | - |
| | Malaysia | Kampung | 1 430 | 55 | 39 |
| | Bangladesh | Local | 1 140 | 40 | 37 |
| | Thailand | Thai | 1 400 | 40 | 48 |
| | Thailand | Betong | 1 900 | 18 | 45 |
| | Thailand | Samae | 2 300 | 70 | - |
| Latin America | Dom. Rep. | Local | 1 500 | 100 | 38 |
| | Bolivia | Local | 1 500 | 100 | - |
| **Intensive** | | | | | |
| Africa | Egypt | Fayoumi | 1 354 | 150 | 43 |
| | Egypt | Dandarawi | - | 140 | 45 |
| | Egypt | Baladi | 1 330 | 151 | 40 |
| | Nigeria | Local | 1 500 | 125 | 36 |
| | United Rep. Tanzania | Local | 1 652 | 109 | 46 |
| | Uganda | Local | 1 500 | 40 | 50 |
| | Zambia | Local | 1 500 | 35 | 52 |
| Asia | Bangladesh | Desi | 1 300 | 45 | 35 |
| | India | Kadakanath | 1 125 | 80 | 40 |
| | Indonesia | Ayam Nunukan | 2 000 | 150 | 48 |
| | Indonesia | Ayam Kampung | 1 350 | 104 | 45 |

Sources: Compiled from Horst, 1989; Katule, 1991; Horst *et al.*, 1996; Haque, 1999.

Domesticated guinea fowl are of three principal varieties: Pearl, White and Lavender. The Pearl is by far the most common. It has purplish-grey feathers regularly dotted or "pearled" with white. The White guinea fowl has pure white feathers while the Lavender has light grey feathers dotted with white. The male and female guinea fowl differ so little in appearance (feather colour and body weight [1.4 to 1.6 kg]) that the inexperienced farmer may unknowingly keep all males or all females as "breeding" stock. Sex can be distinguished at eight weeks or more by a difference in their voice cry.

Domesticated guinea hens lay more eggs under intensive management. French Galor guinea hens can produce 170 eggs in a 36-week laying period. For example, from a setting of 155 eggs, a fertility rate of 88 percent and hatchability of 70 to 75 percent, it is possible to obtain 115 guinea keets (chicks) per hen. In deep litter or confined range conditions, a 24-week laying period can produce 50 to 75 guinea keets per hen.

**Table 2.4** Reproduction and egg characteristics of guinea fowl varieties

| Traits | Variety | | |
|---|---|---|---|
| | Pearl | Lavender | White |
| Age at 1st egg (d) | 196 | 217 | 294 |
| Eggs/hen/year | 51 | 38 | 43 |
| Egg wt (g) | 38 | 37 | 36 |
| Laying (d/yr) | 155 | 114 | 92 |
| Fertility (%) | 53 | 50 | 0.0 |
| Hatchability (%) | 87 | 81 | 0.0 |

Source: Ayorinde, 1987 and Ayorinde *et al.*, 1984.

## Ducks

Ducks have several advantages over other poultry species, in particular their disease tolerance. They are hardy, excellent foragers and easy to herd, particularly in wetlands where they tend to flock together. In Asia, most duck production is closely associated with wetland rice farming, particularly in the humid and subtropics. An added advantage is that ducks normally lay most of their eggs within the three hours after sunrise (compared with five hours for chickens). This makes it possible for ducks to freely range in the rice fields by day, while being confined by night. A disadvantage of ducks (relative to other poultry), when kept in confinement and fed balanced rations, is their high feed wastage, due to the shovel-shape of their bill. This makes their use of feed less efficient and thus their meat and eggs more expensive than those of chickens (Farrell, 1986). Duck feathers and feather down can also make an important contribution to income.

Different breeds of ducks are usually grouped into three classes: meat or general purpose; egg production; and ornamental.

Ornamental ducks are rarely found in the family poultry sector. Meat breeds include the Pekin, Muscovy, Rouen and Aylesbury. Egg breeds include the brown Tsaiya of Taiwan Province of China, the Patero Grade of the Philippines, the Indian Runner of Malaysia and the Khaki Campbell of England. All these laying breed ducks originate from the green-headed Mallard *(Anas platyrhynchos platyrhynchos)*. The average egg production of the egg breeds is approximately 70 percent (hen.day basis). The Indian Runner, Khaki Campbell, Pekin and Muscovy are the most important breeds in rural poultry.

### *The Indian Runner*

This is a very active breed, native to Asia, and ideal for free-range. It is a very good egg layer and needs less water than most other breeds, requiring only a basin in which it can immerse its beak up to the nostrils. It is the most graceful and elegant of all ducks on land with its upright carriage and slim body. It stands at an angle of about 80° to the ground but when startled can be almost perpendicular.

### *The Khaki Campbell*

Originally bred in England, this breed is derived from three breeds: the wild Mallard, the Rouen and the Indian Runner. The female has an overall khaki colour, and the male has a bronze-green head. The female is best known for her prolific egg laying ability, with an average of 90 percent (on a hen/day basis) with an average 73 gram egg weight.

### *The Pekin*

Originally bred in China, this attractive meat breed is favoured by commercial producers throughout the world. It is large and meaty with an upright stance and a broad round head. It has white to lemon-yellow plumage and a yellow skin. It is hardy, a reasonable layer, and grows rapidly. Although timid, it is docile and easily confined by low fences. It is well suited to both large, specialized duck farms and smallholdings. Pekin ducks are the major meat duck breed in Thailand, Malaysia, Philippines, the Democratic People's Republic of Korea and China.

### *The Muscovy*

This is not genetically a duck or a goose, but is more similar to the goose *(Anseridae)*. It eats grass, as do geese, and has a similarly long egg incubation period of 36 days (compared with that of ducks - 28 days). It is popular in areas where there is little wetland rice production, since it does not require swimming water. The female Muscovy is an excellent brooding mother. It is often used as a foster brooder-mother for other species such as ducks, chickens and guinea fowls. It is a poor layer, producing only 30 to 40 eggs per year under extensive management. The male Muscovy can become very large (4.5 to 5.5 kg) while the female is smaller (2.3 to 2.8 kg). The feather colouring is usually a combination of black and white, ranging from mostly black to mostly white. The male has characteristic red fleshy outcrops around the eyes called *caruncles*. The Muscovy is the predominant waterfowl in Africa and Latin America, as it thrives well under free-range conditions. Numbers are increasing in parts of Asia where lean, red meat is popular (Hahn *et al.,* 1995). When mated with breeds of domestic ducks, they produce infertile hybrid offspring ("mule" ducks). These mule ducks are a major source of duck meat in Taiwan Province of China. A three-way cross-system is used for white mule duck production. Firstly, Pekin drakes are crossed with white Tsaiya ducks to produce a cross-bred female line called the Kaiya duck. These are then crossed with large white Muscovy drakes, usually by artificial insemination. The resulting progeny is a mule duck, which is sterile but grows rapidly. It has good carcass composition with more meat and less fat than the Pekin. These three-way crosses have the added advantages of the high egg production of the Tsaiya, the high growth rate of the Pekin and the good carcass quality and meat texture of the Muscovy. Their white feathers are more valuable as down than those of darker-feathered ducks.

**Table 2.5** Duck breeds and their traits

| Breed | Feather Colour | Body weight (kg) | | Egg colour |
|---|---|---|---|---|
| | | Drake | Duck | |
| Pekin | White | 4.1 | 3.6 | White / Blue green |
| Muscovy | Black/White | 4.5 | 3.0 | White / Green cream |
| Indian Runner | White | 2.0 | 1.8 | White / Creamy white |
| Khaki Campbell | Brown/Khaki | 2.0 | 1.8 | White |
| Mallard | " | 1.4 | 1.1 | Blue green / Mottled |

Source: Hahn *et.al.*, 1995

In most tropical countries, there are local duck breeds that have been selected to suit local conditions. They may not perform as well as improved breeds, but they do have the ability to survive and produce well under local extensive and semi-intensive systems. Setioko (1997) described three Indonesian ducks: Tegal, Alabio and Bali. Improved genotypes have been introduced and have either been crossed with local ducks or remained reasonably pure. There was some concern about the ability of the improved genotypes to survive under traditional farming systems. Trials conducted in the Mekong River Delta by The Bin (1996) found that hybrid ducks raised for **meat** in rice fields were more profitable than the local ducks, even though they consumed more feed and cost more to buy initially. However, when raised for **egg** production in rice fields and on canals, the hybrids did not perform as well as the local ducks.

## Geese

Geese are less important in family poultry production, except in China, where mainly local breeds are kept, except for a few European breeds such as the Toulouse and White Roman, imported for cross-breeding purposes. The great variety in breed size of geese permits their use under various management conditions. At the less intensive levels of production preferred by most family producers, smaller-sized birds (weighing approximately 4 kg, such as the Lingxhian or Zie breeds in China) are easier to manage. Geese are high in the broodiness trait, and have a consequent low egg production of 30 to 40 hatching eggs (in three to five laying cycles) per year. At the other extreme are breeds of high fertility (and egg number), which are smaller and are selected specifically for use in breeding flocks for their lack of broodiness. Breeds such as the Zie may lay 70 to 100 eggs annually. The importance of the wide gene pool variety in China is significant for the Asian region in particular and for the world in general.

## Pigeons

Pigeons are scavengers (not fed any supplementary feed) in most countries, living on the roofs of houses and treated as "pets" that do not need to be fed. They appear to prefer homestead compounds to fields. In some countries, they are eaten only for ritual purposes. They normally lay two eggs in a clutch, and the young birds (squabs) hatch after 16 to 17 days. The growing squabs are fed by their mothers on *crop milk*, produced in the mother's crop (first stomach). This enables young squabs to grow very rapidly. They reach maturity in three to five months at a body weight of 200 to 300 g for males, and 150 g for females. Adult pigeons are monogamous for life.

Local pigeons are specific to different regions in the tropics. Africa has five breeds, within which Chad has three local breeds. Asia and the Pacific have five breeds, with local breeds found specific even to the Cook Islands. Latin America and the Caribbean islands have only one breed. Europe has six breeds, two of which come from Belgium.

## Turkeys

These birds are native to Latin America. The breeds kept by rural producers in the tropics usually have black feathers, as distinct from the white-feathered breeds that are raised intensively. Where there are no geese and ostriches, they are the largest birds in the farming system. Body weight ranges from 7 to 8 kg in males and from 4 to 5 kg in hens. They have good meat conformation, produce about 90 eggs per year and have medium to good hatchability. They are more susceptible to disease than either chicken or ducks.

# Chapter 3
# Feed Resources

## INTRODUCTION

A regular supply of low-cost feed, over and above maintenance requirements, is essential for improved productivity in the three farming systems used in family poultry production:

- free-range – poultry roost in trees at night;
- backyard – poultry are confined at night; and
- semi-intensive – poultry are enclosed during the day in a very limited scavenger resource base.

When feed resources are inadequate, a few birds in production are better than more birds just maintained, but without enough food for production.

### Extensive Systems

Farmers attempt to balance stock numbers according to the scavenging feed resources available in the environment in each season. Under the free-range and backyard systems, feed supplies during the dry season are usually inadequate for any production above flock-maintenance level. When vegetation is dry and fibrous, the scavenging resources should be supplemented with sources of minerals, vitamins, protein and energy. Under most traditional village systems, a grain supplement of about 35 g per hen per day is given.

There have been various approaches to utilising a wider base of feed resources for the flock. One is the use of poultry species apart from chicken. Waterfowl, especially ducks, may be distributed throughout the wetland rural areas, where they can feed on such resources as snails and aquatic plants in ponds and lagoons. Another approach is the integration of poultry with the production of rice, vegetables, fish and other livestock. An example is the combination of chicken with cattle, as practised by the Fulani of Nigeria, where the chickens feed on the ticks on the cattle as well as on the maggots growing in the cattle dung. Chickens raised in the cattle kraal (compound) weighed an average of 500 g more than those in the same neighbourhood but outside the kraal (Atteh and Ologbenla, 1993).

### Semi-Intensive System

Under the semi-intensive system, all the nutrients required by the birds must be provided in the feed, usually in the form of a balanced feed purchased from a feed mill. As these are often expensive and difficult to obtain, smallholders use either unconventional feedstuffs or "dilute" the commercial feed by supplementing it with grain by-products (which supply energy and some protein). A well-balanced feed however is difficult to achieve, as grains and plant protein sources (the by-products of a few oil seeds) are becoming increasingly unavailable for livestock, and premixed trace minerals and vitamins are usually too expensive for smallholders. Phosphorus and calcium can be obtained from ashed (burnt and crushed) bones; and calcium from snail shells, fresh or seawater shellfish shells, or limestone deposits. Salt to supply sodium can come from evaporated seawater or land-based rock salt deposits. These mineral sources are rarely used. Feed provided for birds kept under this system is therefore of a much poorer quality (unbalanced by dilution with crop by-products) than under either the extensive or fully intensive system.

## AVAILABLE FEED RESOURCES

The size and productivity of the village flock ultimately depend on the human population and its household waste and crop residues, and on the availability of other scavengable feed resources. There is a clear relationship between egg production and nutrient intake. This is demonstrated in

Bangladesh, where fewer eggs are laid in the rainy season from August to September, but when snails are available in January and February, production increases (ter Horst, 1986). A list of feed resources available to smallholders was compiled from surveys undertaken in Nigeria (Sonaiya, 1995). These feedstuffs were mostly by-products of home food processing and agro-industries, and were similar to those found in other tropical countries.

The Scavengable Feed Resources Base (SFRB) include:

- household cooking waste;
- cereal and cereal by-products;
- roots and tubers;
- oilseeds;
- trees, shrubs (including *Leucaena, Calliandra* and *Sasbenia)* and fruits;
- animal proteins;
- aquatic plants (*Lemna, Azolla* and *Ipomoea aquatica*); and,
- commercially prepared feed.

These resources are described in greater detail in the following section.

## The Scavengeable Feed Resource Base

Gunaratne *et al.* (1993; 1994), Roberts and Senaratne (1992), Roberts *et al.* (1994) and Roberts (1999) have researched and classified the feed resources available for scavenging poultry in Southeast Asia, which they named the Scavengeable Feed Resource Base (SFRB). The SFRB was defined as the total amount of food products available to all scavenging animals in a given area. It depends on the number of households, the types of food crops grown and their crop cultivating and crop processing methods, as well as on the climatic conditions that determine the rate of decomposition of the food products. Seasonal fluctuations in the SFRB occur due to periods of fallow or flooding, cultivation, harvesting and processing. The SFRB includes termites, snails, worms, insects, grain from sowing, harvesting by-products, seeds, grass, fodder tree leaves, water-plants and non-traditional feed materials. The SFRB can only be harvested by scavenging animals, of which poultry are the most versatile, although this varies with species. Several types of poultry scavenging together can make more effective use of this resource.

Keeping poultry under the free-range and backyard systems depends to a large degree on the quality of the feed available from scavenging. Therefore it is essential to know what feed resources are available. For example: a flock of 12 young growing chickens with five productive hens have access to an SFRB of 450 g (dry weight) containing nine percent protein and 2 300 kcal of metabolizable energy (ME)/kg. This supports about 22 percent daily egg production, with about three eggs/clutch, assuming 80 percent of the SFRB was utilized.

### *Methods of estimating SFRB*

The value of the SFRB can be estimated by weighing the amount of daily food product/household waste generated by each family as parameter "H", which is then divided by the proportion of food product/household waste found in the crop of the scavenging bird (assessed visually) as parameter "p" (Roberts, 1999). This is then multiplied by the percentage of households that keep chickens (parameter "c"):

SFRB = H/p(c)

For example, an SFRB measured using the above method in Southeast Asia ranged from 300 to 600 g on a Dry Matter (DM) basis, containing eight to ten percent of vegetable protein and 8.8 to 10.4 megajoules (MJ) of metabolisable energy (ME) per kg (2 100-2 500 kilocalories [kcal] ME per kg) (Prawirokusumo, 1988; Gunaratne *et al.*, 1993 and 1994). The amount of protein and ME in the SFRB was determined by analysis of the crop content. In Sri Lanka, the annual SFRB available to each family was calculated to contain 23 kg of Crude Protein (CP) and 1959 MJ of ME (468 mega [M] cal of ME) (Gunaratne *et al.*, 1993).

In a case study conducted in Sri Lanka, collections of daily waste from 34 households were made on 14 occasions (Gunaratne *et al.*, 1993). The collections were weighed, examined and analysed for approximate composition, calcium and phosphorus. Fifteen scavenging hens were collected late in the morning and slaughtered and their crop and gizzard contents examined and weighed.

The results indicated that the fresh weight of food product/household waste per household averaged 460 ±210 g per day and consisted of:

- 26 percent cooked rice;
- 30 percent coconut residue;
- 8 percent broken rice; and
- 36 percent other (vegetable trimmings, egg shells, bread, dried fish and scraps).

The crop contents are shown below after Table 3.1.

**Table 3.1** Calculated values of SFRB for family flocks in different countries of Southeast Asia

| Country | SFRB as kg DM/year | Source |
|---|---|---|
| Indonesia | 475 | Kingston and Creswell, 1982 |
| Thailand | 390 | Janviriyasopak *et al.*, 1989 |
| Sri Lanka | 195 | Gunaratne *et al.*, 1993 |
| Sri Lanka | 197 | Gunaratne *et al.*, 1994 |

Source: Gunaratne *et al.*, 1993.

The crop contents comprised:

- 72 percent household waste;
- 13 percent grass;
- 8 percent animal matter (earthworms, snails, ants and flies); and
- 7 percent paddy rice.

For composition details of crop contents and food/products household waste, see Table 3.2 below.

Each family flock had access to the food product/household waste from two households, so that on average the amount available to the household flock was 550 g of Dry Matter per day. Daily egg production ranged from 11 to 57 percent, with an average of 30 percent. This did not vary significantly over the 12 months of the study. Chicken body weight at 20 days ranged from 41 to 100 g, and at 70 days from 142 to 492 g. Mortality up to 70 days was 65 percent. Losses were attributed to predators, particularly dogs, cats, mongooses, crows and other birds of prey. More than 90 percent of the hen's day was spent scavenging over a radius of 110 to 175 m. Cattle and goat pens were favourite scavenging areas.

**Table 3.2** Average composition of major feed components and crop content of scavenging hens in Sri Lanka

| Component | DM | CP | EE | CF | Ash | Ca | P |
|---|---|---|---|---|---|---|---|
| | Percent | | | | | mg/g | |
| Food product /household waste | 43.2 | 10.3 | 7.2 | 2.2 | 1.4 | 0.8 | 4.0 |
| Coconut residue | 24.1 | 6.9 | 38.1 | 8.9 | 1.1 | 1.1 | 6.0 |
| Broken rice | 89.9 | 9.0 | 1.3 | 1.5 | 3.2 | 0.5 | 1.4 |
| Crop content | 34.4 | 9.4 | 9.2 | 5.4 | 16.0 | 0.8 | 0.9 |

Source: Gunaratne *et al.*, 1993 and 1994

***Factors affecting the SFRB***

Among the factors determining the size of the SFRB are: climate; number of households; number and type of livestock owned; crops grown; and the religion of the household. This was clearly illustrated in a Sri Lankan study (Gunaratne *et al.,* 1994), where results showed that the total biomass of the scavenging population was proportional to the SFRB. If the available SFRB is exceeded, then production falls (birds die and hens lay fewer eggs). If there is a surplus SFRB (such as a good harvest or fewer birds due to disease or stock sale), then production increases (more chicks and growers survive and more eggs are laid). Hence the SFRB available in a community determines the production potential of the poultry. If the SFRB is known, other factors affecting production can be identified and the benefits of providing additional inputs assessed.

**Table 3.3** Amount of household waste, calculated SFRB and average flock biomass

| Location - Village name | Month | House waste DM (g) | SFRB DM (g) | SFRB CP (g) | Flock biomass CP (g) |
|---|---|---|---|---|---|
| Galgamuwa I | March | 143 | 260 | 20 | 91 |
| Galgamuwa I | Sept | 267 | 834 | 78 | 75 |
| Galgamuwa II | March | 543 | 639 | 63 | 83 |
| Galgamuwa II | Sept | 549 | 603 | 49 | 36 |
| Ibbagamuwa | June | 414 | 575 | 56 | 57 |
| Ibbagamuwa | August | 307 | 365 | 43 | 48 |

Source: Gunaratne *et al.*, 1994

The maximum productive size of the village flock depends on the SFRB. To keep the flock size in balance with the available SFRB, it is necessary to set fewer eggs for incubation, cull unproductive birds and sell stock as soon as they are saleable. Production capacity should also be adjusted to match the seasonal variations in the SFRB. For example, during harvest time, when the SFRB is increased, extra chicks and growers may be reared, but at the end of the dry season birds may need to be culled, sold or consumed. Supplementing the available SFRB with other feed resources can improve the overall quality of the nutrition of the flock and reduce chick mortality. This may then result in more and larger growers, and the expanded flock could then exceed the SFRB. If this happens, then production will fall again until the balance is restored. Feed supplements are only beneficial if they result in increased off-take rather than increased flock size.

## FEED INGREDIENTS

The on-line and CD-ROM versions of the FAO searchable database *Feeds and Feeding* provide a full resource on this topic for all types of livestock, including poultry. The following descriptions may supplement the above source.

### Cereals and cereal by-products

Examples of grains for supplementing scavenging poultry include millet, sorghum, maize, and rice in the form of whole and broken grains.

Amounts supplied are inadequate when using the surveyed estimate of 35 g supplement grain/bird.day (Obi and Sonaiya, 1995). This and the tannin content of sorghum have led to a search for alternative grains and the evaluation of agro-industrial by-products.

***Dehulled rice grain***

This can be used with vegetable and animal protein supplements for all types of poultry. Rough or paddy rice, off-coloured rice and broken rice have been used up to 20 to 30 percent in poultry rations. Rice bran has a moderate quality protein of 10 to 14 percent, approximately 10.4 MJ of

ME/kg (2 500 kcal of ME/kg), and about 11 percent Crude Fibre (CF). It is rich in phosphorus and B vitamins. Because of its high oil content (14 to 18 percent) it easily goes rancid. For this reason it should make up no more than 25 percent of the ration. This also applies to rice polishings. Rice bran usually includes rice polishings, but is often adulterated with rice hulls/husks, which are very high in fibre and silicon, and have a low nutritive value. Nevertheless, rice bran is still an important feed resource.

***Maize starch residue (MSR)***

This is a by-product of the extraction of starch from fermented, wet-milled maize, which is used as a breakfast cereal in West Africa. It usually has more than 16 percent Crude Protein, although the amount varies according to the maize variety and processing method.

***By-products from local breweries and other local industries***

Brewer's grain and yeast have become common ingredients for poultry rations, but the process of drying the wet by-product can be very expensive.

## Legumes and legume by-products

Non-traditional legumes, such as boiled jack bean (*Canavalia ensiformis*) and sword bean (*Canavalia gladiata*), have been shown to be acceptable to laying hens, although they should not form more than ten percent of the ration because the sword bean is of low nutritive value (Udedibie, 1991). Winged bean (*Phosphocarpus tetragonolobus*) contains approximately 40 percent Crude Protein and 14 percent oil, and its overall nutritive value is very similar to that of soybean and groundnut cake for broiler meat chicken (Smith *et al.,* 1984). Winged bean leaf foliage is also acceptable to laying hens. Unless the plant is grown with stake supports, the yield is very low, which makes its cultivation on a large scale less economical. However it is suitable as a feed and fodder crop for smallholder poultry.

***Soybean (Glycine max)***

This crop is being grown increasingly for human consumption. If the cotyledons (fleshy beans) are used for human food, the testa (bean-seed coat) is given to poultry. Raw soybeans heat-treated by boiling for 30 minutes and then fed to scavenging birds in amounts of up to 35 percent of the ration resulted in satisfactory performance in broilers and laying hens. In pullets and layers fed raw soybeans with no heat treatment as 12 percent of the ration, there was a significant reduction in body weight at 20 weeks, as well as a delay of four days in the onset of sexual maturity (as measured by age at the 50 percent egg production). The heat treatment destroys a trypsin (a digestive enzyme present in the intestine of poultry) inhibitor, which, if left intact, prevents digestion of raw soybean.

***Cowpea (Vigna unguiculata)***

This legume crop is grown solely for human consumption in Africa. Its by-products, especially the testa (seed coat), are used as a feed for small ruminants and have also been fed to poultry (Sonaiya, 1995). The testa represents about six percent of the weight of the whole cowpea, but is usually discarded (in West Africa) when the cotyledons are made into a puree for a locally popular fried cake. With its crude protein content of 17 percent, its apparent metabolizable energy (AME) value of 4.2 MJ of AME/kg (1005 kcal AME/kg) and its mineral profile (44 g ash/kg; 9.0 mg Ca/g; 0.9 mg P/g), cowpea testa should be a good feed resource, but the presence of tannin (53 mg/g) and trypsin inhibitor (12.4 units/mg) limits its utilization. Cowpea testa should not make up more than ten percent of the total feed of a poultry ration.

## Roots and tubers

***Cassava (Manihot esculenta)***

This is grown in large quantities in Africa, Asia and Latin America, both for human consumption and as a livestock feed. Cassava and its by-products (in the form of leaves, small tubers, pulp, peels, chaff, *gari* [fermented grated tubers], *gari* sievings, whole fermented roots and ensiled cassava meal) are used. The dried chips are high in energy and fibre but low in protein. In regions where cassava is used for human food, the peels are the most useful part of the cassava plant for feeding livestock. Amounts of 20 to 45 percent cassava peel meal (CPM) have been fed to chickens, but its use is limited because of the high content of the poison hydrogen cyanide (HCN), as well as high Crude Fibre, low protein content and dust. There is a considerable range of HCN levels in cassava, according to variety. When cassava completely replaces grains in a ration, there is a consequent reduction in egg weight and a change in egg yolk colour. Whether or not there are negative effects on egg fertility and hatchability is not known. Cassava meal gives good growth in meat chickens, although protein and other nutrients must be carefully balanced. Molasses or sugar may be added to sweeten the bitterness of the cyanide and thus improve palatability. Oilseeds such as full fat soybean can compensate for the high fibre and low protein content and for the dustiness. To remove the cyanide, detoxification methods include ensiling, sun-drying, air-drying, roasting, boiling and soaking. For smallholders, the most practical method is sun-drying (Sonaiya and Omole, 1977). Palm oil can also moderate the effects of cyanide on poultry. Some "sweet" varieties of cassava (which do not contain cyanide) are used in human food preparation, and these are often fed to poultry, particularly ducks.

***Sweet potato (Ipomoea batatas)***

Dried sweet potato forming up to 35 percent of the ration has been fed successfully to broilers and layers. The tubers are boiled before use, which overcomes any problems with dust or fungal growth from storage.

## Oilseeds

Oilseeds in full-oil or partly oil-extracted form are a source of both energy and protein for extensive and intensive poultry systems.

***Cotton (Gossypium spp.)***

Glanded cotton seed cake (CSC) is a high-demand supplement fed to ruminants, but if available it can be fed in amounts up to 25 percent in the diets of layers and broilers without adversely affecting egg production and growth (Branckaert, 1968). Poultry are tolerant of the gossypol found in CSC, but it can cause an olive discolouration of egg yolks, which consumers do not like. Addition of 0.25 percent ferrous sulphate should be added routinely to laying hen rations containing up to ten percent CSC.

***Sesame (Sesamum indicum)***

The feed consumption and conversion rates for birds fed various forms of raw unhulled sesame seeds were better than those for birds fed dehulled but whole sesame seeds, confirming the practice of smallholders who use whole sesame seeds as a supplement for scavenging poultry. Sesame seeds should used in amounts between 20 and 35 percent of the ration.

***Groundnuts (Arachis hypogaea)***

Groundnuts may be used in the oil-extracted cake form to make up 8 to 24 percent of the ration. Mouldy groundnuts may contain toxic substances, the most dangerous of which is aflatoxin.

***Coconut (Cocos nucifera)***

Coconut meal can be used to form 50 percent of the ration, especially when combined with a high-energy source such as cassava meal. It is low in lysine, isoleucine, leucine and methionine.

***Sunflower (Helianthus Annuus)***

Sunflower seeds can be fed whole, or the decorticated meal can be used to replace groundnut cake and soybean meal and up to two-thirds of fishmeal. It has the highest sulphur amino acid content of all the major oilseeds.

***Oil Palm (Elaeis guineensis)***

Most oil palms are processed locally. The by-products are kernels and an aqueous solution of oil, fibre and solids. This solution can be filtered to remove the fibre (which is used as fuel). This leaves an aqueous mixture called palm oil sludge (POS), which supplies feed energy and fatty acids. Sludge processed using chemical solvents should not be used, as the chemical residue may be toxic to the birds. It can be fermented and used in smallholder poultry systems or dried to form up to 40 percent of commercial compound feeds (Hutagalang, 1981). Palm kernels are processed locally into palm kernel oil by heat or cold-water extraction. The residue from heat extraction is similar to ash and of no use in poultry feed, but the residue from water extraction is very nutritious and palatable to birds, and can be used in the same way as groundnut cake. The meal can provide up to 30 percent of the ration. However, the product is low in the sulphur amino acids.

***Soybean – see under Legumes and legume by-products***

***Other oilseeds***

Other oilseeds that have been fed to poultry under research conditions include rubber, amaranth, Niger seed (*Nueg*), breadfruit *(Artocarpus altilis)*, locust bean *(Ceratonia siliqua)*, African oil bean, melon, mango and castor oil. Okra seed *(Hibiscus esculentus)* has not yet been evaluated as a protein source for poultry, and although it is lower in protein, it compares favourably with soybean in all other nutrient components. Since okra is widely grown by smallholders and the seeds are kept for planting, it may be a potential source of protein for smallholder poultry.

***Bambara groundnut (Voandzeia subterranea)***

This is a good source of protein with a high lysine content. As the nut is not widely eaten, the plant is grown mainly as a mulch crop and the foliage is scavenged by poultry.

## Trees, shrubs and fruits

***Neem leaves***

A pilot study was undertaken to test the response of three groups of layers to neem leaves. One group was fed a ration containing ten per cent fresh neem leaves, the second a ration of ten per cent dried neem leaves, and the third none. The group receiving the fresh neem leaves had increased feed intake, daily egg production and egg weight compared with the other two. There appears to be a fat component of fresh neem leaves *(Azadirachta indica)* that enhances egg production and egg weight (Siddiqui *et al.*, 1986).

***Coffee pulp***

This is high in fibre, but as the essential amino acid content is similar to that of soybean, it can only be used in limited amounts.

***Citrus pulp***

No more than two percent citrus pulp should be included in the ration to avoid reduction in growth rate and off-colour egg yolks.

***Over-ripe bananas and plantains***

These are of greater palatability for poultry than green bananas, which contain free or active tannins.

***Derinded sugarcane pith and molasses***

Sugarcane juice can make up to 25 percent of the poultry ration and molasses up to 30 percent, but it should be noted that over ten percent molasses results in watery faeces. Raw sugar however can be fed at up to 50 percent of the ration without watery faeces. Combining one part molasses with three parts sugar gives good production without the digestive problems. Molasses is often added to rations at low levels of inclusion to make it more palatable, although there may be problems with evenly mixing the liquid, and with fungal toxins in the stored feed, encouraged by the sugar levels.

**Table 3.4** Optimum levels of inclusion in poultry rations of some ingredients

| Feedstuff | Optimum level in the diet (%) |
|---|---|
| Banana meal | 5-10 |
| Citrus molasses | 5-10 |
| Citrus pulp | 1-2 |
| Cocoa bean residue | 2-7 |
| Cocoa husk | 6-15 |
| Cocoa shell | 5-15 |
| Coconut meal/cake | 5-15 |
| Coffee grounds | 3-5 |
| Coffee pulp | 3-5 |
| Kapok seed cake | 5-10 |
| Leucaena leaf meal | 2-5 |
| Oil-palm sludge, dried | 10-30 |
| Oil palm sludge, fermented | 20-40 |
| Palm kernel meal | 10-40 |
| Palm oil | 2-8 |
| Rubber seed meal | 10-30 |
| Sugar cane molasses | 10-30 |
| Raw sugar | 40-50 |
| Sugar cane juice | 10-25 |

Source: Hutagalung, 1981

## Animal protein

***Blood meal***

This is recognized as a high crude protein source with an imbalanced, relatively poor amino acid profile. Handling and processing of blood is difficult in low-technology situations. For processing small amounts, one method is to absorb the blood on a vegetable carrier such as citrus meal, brewers grain, palm kernel, ground maize, cob rice or wheat bran, after which the material is spread out for drying on trays heated from below or placed in the sun (Sonaiya, 1989). At the farm level, the blood may be supplied from the slaughter of livestock. Abattoirs and slaughterhouses provide large volumes of blood for making up feeds at the commercial level.

***Termites***

Farina, *et al.*, (1991) described a technique used to collect termites for scavenging poultry. Briefly, the straw of sorghum, millet and maize are chopped, placed in clay pots or calabashes and moistened. The mouth of the container is placed over a hole in a termite colony under construction. The container is covered with a jute sack to prevent drying out and a heavy stone is placed on it to secure it in position. After three to four weeks, a new colony of termites should be established inside the container. The eggs and larvae are particularly relished by chicks, guinea keets and ducklings, while adult birds also feed on the adult insects. Cattle dung can be used in place of the cereal straw.

### *Maggots*

Alao and Sonaiya (1991) grew maggots on cowpea testa (seed coats) and monitored the chemical composition of the mixture over ten days. Cowpea testa samples were placed in a basket near a pit latrine to attract flies to lay eggs on them. Every two days, a sample was steeped in boiling water to kill the maggots. They were then sun-dried and ground before analysis. Results showed that the Crude Protein content of the mixture doubled by the second day. Soukossi (1992) produced maggots from fibrous vegetable material and poultry droppings. The method was developed for feeding fish, but can easily be adapted for smallholder poultry. A tank with a capacity of one cubic metre is filled with water to about 15 cm from the top. Dried stalks of maize, amaranth, groundnut, soya and other legumes are soaked in the water to which some poultry droppings are added. Flies and other insects are attracted to the soaked material to lay their eggs. After five to seven days, eggs are hatched and larvae are sufficiently developed to be fed to fish. Beyond this period the maggots develop into adult flies. It was observed that up to 50 percent of the eggs laid by flies died if exposed to the sun for several hours. A cover, at least for the hottest hours of the day, is therefore necessary. Similar trials have been carried out in Burkina Faso.

### *Earthworms*

Vorster *et al.* (1992) produced earthworms as a source of protein for chicken feed. In an area of 25 $m^2$, one kg of fresh earthworm biomass was produced daily. This is sufficient to supplement at least 50 chickens with high-quality protein. It must be noted, however, that earthworms (and snails as well) may be important vectors for tapeworms such as *Davainea* and *Raillietina* and also contain a growth inhibitor.

### *Other animal products*

Aquatic animal products containing mineral sources include marine shells from mangrove oysters (*Ostrea tulipa),* mangrove periwinkles *(Tympanostomus fuscatus)* and clams, and shells from land snails. Marine shells are abundantly available in coastal areas. Snails and their shells are harvested from forests, but there is also on-going development of productive snail farms. It is estimated that a box with a capacity of one cubic metre capacity on a snail farm can yield 40 snails each year. Ducks are an important biological control of the semi-aquatic golden snail in the Philippines and Bangladesh. Other marine by-products, such as prawn dust and shrimp heads, supply both minerals and protein.

## CONCLUSIONS

There are feed resources available for feeding poultry at all levels of production. Smallholders using the semi-intensive system who make their own feed must base the rations on home-produced feed resources or obtain the ingredients locally. In backyard systems, available resources should be supplemented with appropriate nutrients as necessary. Food products from household waste fed to free-range birds should also be supplemented. Potential substitutes for expensive commercial feeds are cassava, sweet potato, coco yam *(Colocasia esculenta),* arrowroot *(Marantha arundinacea),* coconut residues, coconut oil, palm oil and other non-traditional energy sources. Non-conventional feedstuffs which are good substitutes for fish meal and soybean and groundnut oil meals include earthworm meal, maggot meal, winged bean, pigeon pea, jack bean, *Azolla (A. pinnata, A. caroliniana, A. microphylla)*, leaf meals and leaf protein concentrates.

In different regions, the importance of these feed resources for family poultry depends on their availability in sufficient quantities for farm use, simple preparation and processing

**methods, knowledge of the potential nutritive values and (for comparison) the price and availability of conventional commercial feeds.**

**For the family poultry situation with a scavenger flock, free-choice supplements with three containers each containing either protein-rich, energy-rich or mineral-rich feed sources will provide a solution to the problem of balancing nutrient intake for different age-groups. Poultry have an instinctual ability to select exactly what they need in the above food nutrient groups, and will not overeat from any one container. Young growing poultry (under two months of age) should always be fed in a "creep" system, where older stock cannot get access to their feed supply.**

# Chapter 4
# General Management

## HOUSING AND RUNS

Under undomesticated conditions, poultry lay eggs in simple nests, perch in trees and spend much of the day scavenging for feed. Chickens spend a large proportion of their time scratching to expose hidden food. Under the backyard and semi-intensive production systems, poultry are usually enclosed at night to discourage thieves and predators, and under intensive production, are totally confined day and night. Some village households keep their few chickens inside the house or even under their bed at night, to discourage theft.

Given a choice of a place to lay their eggs, hens will choose a soft "litter" base, and they prefer an adequately sized (a cube of approximately 30 cm), darkened nest with some privacy. Prior to laying, hens usually investigate a number of possible sites before entering a nest box. They then show nesting behaviour, which includes a special protective nest-seeking voice, after which they sit and finally lay. When they have laid an egg, they announce this with another type of "pride of achievement" call. These calls can also be heard in a battery cage house. If perches are provided, hens will perch most of the time rather than stand on the wire floors, and after dark most birds roost on the perches. Perching is a probable survival characteristic to avoid night predators. The basic requirements for poultry housing are:

- space;
- ventilation;
- light; and
- protection (from weather and predators).

### Space: density of birds per unit area

This is the most important basic principle in housing, as the space available determines the number and type of poultry that can be kept. For example, a deep litter house measuring 6 m by 11 m can hold 200 laying hens at a stock density of 3 birds/$m^2$ (3.6 $ft^2$/bird). Under the older system of measuring, stock density was measured in $ft^2$ per bird, which is the inverse of birds per $m^2$ used in the metric system, incorporating a conversion factor of 0.0929 $m^2/ft^2$ (for details, see the appendix entitled Abbreviations and Conversions).

Linear space or length of perch per bird is measured in centimetres. The recommended floor and perching space for the three main types of chicken is shown in Table 4.1.

**Table 4.1** Requirement of chickens for floor and perch space

| Chicken types | Floor Space (birds/$m^2$) | Floor Space ($ft^2$/bird) | Perch Space (per bird) |
|---|---|---|---|
| Layer | 3 | 3.6 | 25 cm (10 in) |
| Dual Purpose | 4 | 2.7 | 20 cm (8 in) |
| Meat | 4-5 | 2.1-2.7 | 15-20 cm (6-8 in) |

Hen groups are comfortable at a stock density of three to four birds per square metre. If more space is allowed, a greater variety of behaviour can be expressed. Less space creates stressed social behaviour, allowing disease vulnerability and cannibalism and leaving weaker birds deprived of feed or perch space. Individual birds need more room for normal behaviour and adequate exercise than the 22 birds/$m^2$ (0.5 $ft^2$/bird) density currently used in commercial laying cages. Over recent decades, animal welfare concerns have encouraged research on laying cage structures to make designs better suited to the needs of hens, while retaining cost-effectiveness for production.

### Ventilation: air flow

Ventilation is an important factor in housing. A building with open sides is ideal, otherwise cross-ventilation at bird-level should be allowed for in the form of floor level inlets, open in a direction to allow the prevailing wind to blow across the width of the building. An air mass between the side walls of a poultry house resists being moved, even across an open-sided building. The wider the building, the more the resistant it is to air movement. Buildings over 8 m (26 ft) wide have a significantly greater problem because of this inherent property of air to resist movement. It is recommended that buildings relying on natural airflow for ventilation should not exceed 8 m in width.

Heat stress is a significant constraint to successful production and can lead to death. Although birds can withstand several degrees below freezing, they do not tolerate temperatures over 40 °C. This depends on the relative humidity prevailing at the time. Poultry do not possess sweat glands and must cool themselves by panting out water in their breath, which is evaporative cooling. When the humidity is too high, this cooling mechanism does not work very well. Lethal temperatures for most chickens are 46 °C upwards, and severe stress sets in above 40 °C. In temperate regions, the chicken house may be constructed to face the rising morning sun to gain heat. In the tropics however, an east-west orientation of the length of the building helps to minimize exposure to direct sunlight. Building materials such as tin or other metal should be avoided for this reason, although white paint will reflect up to 70 percent of incident solar heat radiation. Ventilation concerns in building alignment may prevail over solar heat control in this aspect, as cross-flow ventilation requires the side of the building to face the prevailing wind.

Ground cover can also reduce reflected heat. Shade should be provided, especially if there is little air movement or if humidity is high. With no shade, or when confined in higher temperatures, poultry become heat stressed and irritable, and may begin to peck at one another. When new pinfeathers are growing (especially on young stock), blood is easily drawn, which can lead to cannibalism. The effects of heat stress are:

- a progressive reduction in feed intake as ambient temperature rises;
- an increase in water consumption in an attempt to lower temperature;
- a progressive reduction in growth rate; and
- disturbances in reproduction (lower egg weight, smaller chicks, reduced sperm concentration and an increased level of abnormal sperm in cocks).

### Light: duration and intensity

A well-lit house is essential. A dark house leads to lethargic, inactive, unproductive birds. Light is important for feeding, as poultry identify food by sight. This is especially important for intensively managed day-old chicks, which need very bright 24-hour lighting for their first week of life.

Light is also an important factor in sexual maturity. An increasing light proportion in the day, as naturally occurs from mid-winter to mid-summer, will accelerate sexual maturity in growing pullets, bringing them to lay sooner. If hens are already laying, the increasing light proportion will increase egg production. The opposite effect is also true: as the light proportion of the day decreases (as naturally occurs from mid-summer to mid-winter), then sexual maturity is slowed in growing stock, and egg production is reduced in laying hens. These effects are somewhat reduced towards the equator, as the difference in the daylight proportion of a day changes less and less.

This physiological effect on poultry is important in terms of maintaining egg production in commercial flocks, and requires supplementary lighting programmes. Regular and reliable electricity supply is required for such programmes, otherwise the effect can be made worse by breaks in the light supplementation system. A slow but steady increase maximises the rate of production. However, lighting programmes producing an effective daylight proportion in excess of 17 hours per day can have a worsening effect on egg production. A 24-hour security lighting system can have such an effect on egg production.

Birds do best in situations where there is plenty of natural light that does not raise the temperature of the house. Natural light is preferable unless regular, reliable and well-distributed artificial light can be provided. It is recommended that the interior of the house be whitewashed to reflect light. The intensity or brightness of the light is also important. Egg production will decrease at light intensities lower than five lux (the "lux" is the metric unit of light intensity and can be measured by a meter similar to that measuring light intake into a camera lens), although meat chicken will keep growing optimally at light intensities as low as two lux (not bright enough to read a newspaper). These intensities are measured at the eye-level of the bird, not near the light source. Unless supplementary lighting is spaced uniformly, there may be areas in the building insufficiently lit to allow optimum growth or egg production. Designs for layout assume that the light bulbs or tubes will be kept clean, as dusty surfaces will reduce light output.

### Protection: shelter sheds and buildings

Many factors influence the type and choice of housing to protect poultry from the effects of weather and predators. These include the local climate, the available space, the size of the flock and the management system. In extensive systems, birds must be protected from disease and predators but also be able to forage. Traditional large animal fencing using live plants is not enough protection against predators such as snakes, kites, rats and other vermin.

A simple and effective system to deter predator birds is to tie parallel lines of string across the main scavenging area, the intervals between which measure less than the predator's wingspan; or, alternatively, a fishing net supported on poles can be spread across the side of the run where predator birds could swoop on the scavenging chicks.

Leg traps can be set for large predators. It is not necessary to set traps around all the pens, as predators tend to attack the same pen on the second night. Steel traps can be boiled in walnut hulls or cocoa pods, both to camouflage them and to prevent rust. The traps will be more effective if not touched with bare hands, as most predators have a keen sense of smell. Instead, they should be handled with a stick, rubber gloves or tongs.

Rats, mongooses and snakes are only a problem when the birds are small. Rats often come up through the earth floors, and the first signs of a rat attack may be unusually quiet chicks huddled under the brooder heater or in a corner, or dead chicks with small bloody neck scratches. Snakes will kill chicks if they can get into the brooder house. A treble fishhook in a dead bird can be left as bait: the snake will swallow the hooks as it gulps down the bird and eventually die. Holes around doors and windows through which rats and snakes may enter should be plugged.

Coops or baskets may be used to house mother hens and chicks in order to reduce chick mortality due to predators, thieves and rain. They also allow for separate feed and water supplementation, although the inadequate feed usually provided in coops means that some scavenging remains necessary.

**Table 4.2** Predator attack modes and control methods

| Predator | Attack mode | Control method |
|---|---|---|
| Hawk | Picks up stray birds and weaklings. Attacks birds so that head and toe marks are visible on back. Often plucks birds. | Hunt the hawk and keep chicks away from clear swoop areas. |
| Rat, mongoose | Usually take more than they eat, and stuff chicks in holes for later consumption. | If allowed, use rat poison. |
| Snake | Will swallow eggs and chicks | Use fishhooks. |
| Dog, cat | General destruction | Try to catch them. Cats can control rats but wild cats and dogs are a problem. |
| Fox, jackal | Will bite off the feathers over the back and between wings, eat the entrails and breast, and carry bird to den. | Roam in the early morning; kill for their young. Trapping is the best control. |
| Raccoon | Pulls off head and eats crop. Will carry birds off. | May be protected in some countries. A permit to destroy may be required. |

## HOUSING IN FREE-RANGE SYSTEMS

Overnight shelter which is roomy, clean and airy should be provided under free-range systems. Houses may be either fixed or mobile. If space permits, a mobile chicken house may be appropriate, and to increase egg production, mobile folds or field units for laying birds can be provided. These mobile units can be rotated on the range. Although housing is cheaper and there is less need for balanced rations, the birds are exposed to the sun and prone to parasite infestation.

The stocking density on pasture should be calculated according to the soil type and pasture management system. A night shelter for up to 20 free-range chickens can be attached to any existing structure, such as the farmer's outhouse, kitchen or dwelling. In a deep litter system, there should be a density of at most three to four birds per square metre. In regions where it rains heavily, the floor should be raised with a generous roof overhang, particularly over the entrance. The raised floor can be a solid platform of earth or a raised bamboo platform. The raised bamboo platform has the advantage of providing ventilation under the poultry, which helps cool them in hot weather and keeps them out of flood water in the monsoons.

The walls of the building can be made of mud or bamboo, and the windows and door of bamboo slats. The house can also be free-standing, and may also be suitable for semi-intensive or intensive production systems.

## HOUSING IN SEMI-INTENSIVE AND INTENSIVE SYSTEMS

### Planning

Complete confinement is only advisable where:

- there is good management;
- reproduction is spread equally over the year;
- land is scarce or inaccessible all year round;
- balanced rations are available;
- a supply of hybrid day-old chicks is available;
- labour is expensive;
- parasite and disease control are readily available; and
- the objective is commercial production.

The reasons for confinement are, in order of priority, to:

- reduce mortality due to predation in chicks under two months of age;

- achieve higher daily gain and better feed conversion in growers; and
- allow better supervision of production in laying hens.

In all confined systems, the location and building design must be carefully considered. The area surrounding the house should be mown or grazed. A good location should meet the following criteria:

- It should be easily accessible.
- There should be a reliable water supply.
- The ground should be well drained.
- It should be at a sufficient distance from residential areas (far enough to protect human health and close enough to provide security for the birds).
- It should be well away from woodland.

Converting existing facilities can provide housing, although planning permission may have to be obtained. An unused outhouse kitchen, for example, can be converted into a poultry house. In all conversions, maximum use should be made of the space available through careful planning:

- A plan of the building should be drawn to scale.
- Use should be made of existing floors and walls, if suitable.
- Space requirements of the birds and manure disposal should be taken into consideration.
- A feasibility study should be carried out, taking into consideration future plans and requirements as well as the economics of converting the building.

## Construction

The floor is extremely important. An ideal floor for a deep litter house is well drained and made of concrete, with a layer of heavy gravel or wire mesh embedded in it to keep out rats. This type of floor is usually costly. Wood, bamboo, bricks or large flat stones (according to what is locally available) can be used, but are harder to clean. Clay floors are cheaper, but require the application of a fresh layer of clay either between flock batches or at least annually. In areas where construction materials are cheaper than deep litter, and particularly in humid regions where litter material is not available, raised floors are sometimes used. These are made of wire mesh, expanded metal, wooden slats or split bamboo, to allow the droppings to collect under the house, and should be about one metre above the ground to allow for cleaning and ventilation. Higher floors may result in an unstable building. They are supported by pillars, which are either rot-resistant or have stone or concrete footings, and which are made of such materials as wood, bamboo, oil drums and conorete blocks. Houses with raised floors on posts can be protected against rats with baffles. The baffles can be made of a metal collar, a tin can turned upside-down or a metal band wound around the post, but must fit tightly to deter even the smallest rodent.

The roof and walls of the house can be made of any inexpensive local material, including bamboo slats, sorghum stalks, mud, wooden slats and palm fronds, as long as the structure is made relatively rat-proof. In colder regions, the walls should be thicker or insulated, but in warmer climates thatch can be used, although it should be replaced frequently to minimize parasite and disease problems. The inside of the walls should be as smooth as possible, to prevent tick and mite infestation and to make cleaning easier. Interior length-ways building partitions are not advisable, as they reduce cross-flow ventilation.

The roof should be watertight, and should overhang the walls by one metre if the windows have no shutters. The roof can be made of thatch, sheet metal or tiles. Thatch is usually the cheapest option and provides good insulation. It will probably have to be replaced every three years, or immediately if ticks get into it. It should be interlaced with bamboo or wooden slats to keep predators out. Sheet metal is usually too expensive, and in hot climates must be painted with white or aluminium to reflect sun heat. However, it is easily cleaned which is an important advantage where ticks are a problem. A layer of plastic sheeting sandwiched between bamboo slats is a good seal against rain and vermin. Flattened oil drums can be used at a lower cost. Although usually more expensive than thatch, sun- or oven-baked tiles will last much longer. Because of their weight, the frame for a tiled roof must be stronger than for other materials.

Window design depends on the local climate. Chickens need more ventilation than humans, but should be sheltered from wind, dust and rain. During storms, wood or bamboo hinged shutters or curtains made from feed sacks can cover window openings on the windward side of the house. In humid climates, window design should take as much advantage of the wind direction as possible to reduce the amount of moisture in the house. Window areas are best covered by wire mesh or expanded metal. Wooden slats or bamboo can be used, depending on available funds and materials. However, the thicker the material, the more ventilation will be reduced. Doors should be made of metal, wood or bamboo. The top half of the door could be wire mesh. Doors should be sufficiently strong to withstand being opened and closed many times a year.

Gabled roofs reduce solar heat loading when compared with flat or lean-to roofs. The pitch or "angle of rise" on a gabled roof is important for many reasons. Traditional village thatched gabled roofs are usually constructed using bush timber, and at a steeply pitched angle (greater than 42° from the horizontal), which helps the roof to withstand stormy winds. Shallower pitched roofs are more susceptible to being blown off in strong winds, particularly when the pitch angle is 15° to 20°. Shallower pitched roofs have less roof surface area, which reduces the cost of surfacing material, but because they are more affected by stormy winds, they need stronger support frames, which results in a much higher overall roof cost. A 42° pitch is the optimum compromise between roof surfacing costs and roof support costs.

The maximum width for an open-sided poultry building, under conditions of a slight breeze, which allows air movement across the shed at the height of the bird, is 8 m (26 ft). To maximise the volume and velocity of airflow across the shed width, the end walls of the shed should be closed. This forces the air to flow across the shed width, especially if the wind is not already coming from that side. Centre ridge ventilation is not recommended, as it discourages airflow across the full shed width. Air enters at the prevailing wind side and is drawn up at the centre to exit at the ridge, excluding the other half of the building.

## Nests

To avoid excessive competition and minimize eggs laid on the floor, one nest should be provided for every five hens. If larger communal nests are used, at least one square metre per 50 birds should be allowed. Baskets, pots and cardboard boxes can be used for nests. Dimensions suitable for a basket or pot nest are a 25 cm base diameter, 18 cm high walls, and a 40 cm open top diameter. Nests should be situated in a secure, shady secluded place out of the sun, lined with fresh litter and kept clean. Nest boxes for individual hens should be constructed in multiple groups for larger numbers of hens. These are usually made of wood, and should measure approximately 30 cm on all sides, with a nest floor area of about 0.1 $m^2$.

## Perches and roosts

Chickens prefer to roost at night on perches. Perching space of 15 to 20 cm should be allowed for each bird. Birds lower in the social peck order can also use the perches during the day. The cross-section of each perch bar should be 2 to 3 cm. Their length depends upon the number of birds to be housed. The perches should be placed within a frame, and aligned parallel to the wall, and horizontally, with a sliding, removable platform called the "droppings board" about 20 cm below the perches to catch the manure droppings. The first perch bar should be placed 20 to 25 cm out from the back wall, and subsequent ones at 30 to 40 cm intervals. The droppings board should touch the back wall and extend 30 cm in front of the front perch bar, as this will allow the birds to land from their flight from the floor before seeking a perching spot. Droppings boards should be a maximum of 75 cm from the floor of the house, and the perch bars should be about 20 cm above the droppings board, to facilitate cleaning of the droppings board. Fowls deposit over half their droppings at night, and the use of the droppings boards thus helps to keep the floor clean. The manure can then be easily collected, dried and stored in empty feed sacks for use as an excellent fertilizer for plants requiring organic nitrogen. The area under the droppings board then becomes an ideal site for a communal nest.

## Providing feed

In both intensive and semi-intensive systems, laying hens need constant access to food and water, and feeders should be distributed evenly throughout the chicken house. In the semi-intensive system, birds scavenge during the day, mostly for protein (from such sources as insects, worms and larva), minerals (from stones, grits and shells), and vitamins (from leafy greens, oil palm and nuts), but energy supplements such as maize, sorghum and millet are important for higher productivity and should be given. Chapter 3 on Feed Resources discusses ingredients and feeding systems in more detail.

### *Feeders*

A good feeder should be:

- durable enough to withstand frequent cleaning;
- stable enough not to be knocked over;
- of the correct height and depth;
- bird proof (such that birds cannot get into it or roost in it); and
- equipped with a lip to prevent birds from spooning feed out onto the floor with their beaks.

The height of the feed inside the feeder, which should never be more than one-third full, should be level with the back of the birds, to prevent them from scratching contaminated litter into the feeders and to limit feed wastage. This is achieved by adjusting the height of the feeder itself. To reduce spoilage and mould problems, feed should be supplied at sunrise and at about 14.00 hours (or more frequently if the birds empty the feeder), with all feed finished by sundown. Feeders can be made of wood, sheet metal or bamboo, and are best suspended from the roof to keep rats out. The height of the feeder should be adjustable. Supplementary vegetable matter should be fed at beak level, either hanging from the ceiling wrapped in a string or placed in a net or placed in a floor-standing hopper with wire or slatted sides. It should not be thrown on the floor.

Feeder space is measured as the linear distance of lip available to the birds. This is either the circumference of a round tube-feeder tray or twice the length of a trough if the birds feed from both sides. If troughs are used, at least 10 cm of feeding space should be accessible to each bird. When circular feeders are used, there should be at least 4 cm feeding space per bird.

**Table 4.3** Feed and feeder space requirements for 100 chickens

| Age (weeks) | Daily feed consumption (kg) | Suggested feeder depth (cm) | Feeder space (m) |
|---|---|---|---|
| 1 – 4 | 1.4 - 5.0 | 5 | 2.5 |
| 4 – 6 | 3.2 - 7.3 | 8 | 3.8 |
| 6 – 9 | 5.0 - 9.5 | 9 | 6.1 |
| 10 – 14 | 7.3 - 15.9 | 12.5 | 9.6 |
| 15 and above | 9.1 - 11.4 | 15 | 12.7 |

### *Creep Feeders*

Creep feeders are used to enable baby chicks to have access (by "creeping" through a small doorway) to high-quality (high in energy and protein) feed, while blocking access to larger sized birds (especially the chicks' mothers). The conical (open at the top and base) creep feeder can be made from split bamboo strips approximately 0.5 to 1 cm wide, bound at the joints with string or wire. The base of the creep feeder can be 75 cm in diameter and 70 cm high, with an access hole (reinforced to form a carrying handle as well) about 20 cm wide at the top. The gaps between the upright slats can be 2 to 3 cm at the bottom and about 1 cm at the top. The flexibility of the bamboo strips allows the size of the entryways to be enlarged, as the chicks grow bigger. If the chicks are reluctant to leave their mothers' side, then a more tightly formed weave can prevent their exit once they are placed inside the cone through an opening at the top. The bamboo can be preserved from insect attack with a coat of used engine oil.

Better nutrition for young stock boosts their immune response to disease challenge and to vaccine response by developing full immunity. Gunaratne *et al* (1994) reported that chick mortality rates could be reduced by the use of creep feeders but that this did not increase the growth rate. However, when the household waste was supplemented with protein and fed in the creep feeder, both the growth and the survival rate of chicks increased (Roberts *et al.*, 1994).

Table 4.4 shows that annual egg production can be doubled because of the increased laying time available to the hens if their chicks are fed in a creep feeder after hatching (Pratseyo *et al.*, 1985). If the gaps in the creep feeder are adjusted, it can also be used for growers over eight weeks, and if given less than the full ration, they will learn to compete for food with other chickens.

**Table 4.4** The effect of creep feeding on flock egg production

| Intervention | Period | | | | | |
|---|---|---|---|---|---|---|
| | June | July | Aug. | Sept. | Oct. | Nov. |
| Creep only | 31.5 | 28.7 | 27.3 | 21.8 | 21.4 | 33.0 |
| Creep + Low supplement | 21.2 | 18.8 | 22.9 | 26.9 | 30.7 | 31.1 |
| Creep + High supplement | 24.3 | 24.5 | 32.5 | 34.1 | 27.4 | 31.1 |

Source: Gunaratne *et al.*, 1993

## Providing water

Providing clean water is a priority often neglected. The amount of water, the right type of equipment and where it is situated are important considerations. Table 4.5 shows water consumption rates for hot dry conditions, and these can be halved for temperate regions.

**Table 4.5** Minimum water and watering space requirements for 100 birds in hot dry conditions

| Age (weeks) | Daily consumption (litres) | Water space (m) |
|---|---|---|
| 0 – 1 | 3 | 0.7 |
| 2 – 4 | 10 | 1.0 |
| 4 – 9 | 20 | 1.5 |
| 9 or more | 25 | 2.0 |
| Layer | 50 | 2.5 |

In countries with plenty of water, such as Bangladesh, Viet Nam, Indonesia, the Gambia, Sierra Leone, Zaire and Uganda, the only special measure to be taken is to ensure its cleanliness. In other regions, especially in the Sahel and other drought-prone regions, fetching and carrying water is a crucial task, usually assigned to women and children. In the rainy season, clean water and feed must be placed in the house, as brooding hens are kept inside to prevent poor hatchability resulting from contamination with mud and dirt.

The simplest equipment is a tin can inverted into a soup plate or the bottom of a larger tin can. A hole is punched about 2 cm from the open end of the tin can. The can is filled with water, covered with the plate and both quickly inverted. The position of the punched hole and the vacuum in the tin can will regulate the water level in the plate. Tin can waterers work well but quickly become rusty, especially in the humid tropics. A clay pot or gourd with holes around the sides sunk into the ground for stability can be used to water adult birds. Clay pots of any dimension can often be ordered from local pot makers. Because they are permeable they provide water half a degree Celsius cooler than other waterers, as heat loss through evaporation keeps the water cooler. This also means an appreciable loss of water over time, especially in very hot dry areas, so that the pots may have to be made more impermeable by glazing. If continuous drinking troughs are used, at least 5 cm of trough should be allowed for each bird. Alternatively, one cup or nipple drinker may be provided for every ten birds.

## BABY CHICK MANAGEMENT

Baby chicks should be kept warm and dry. The nest, which they share at night with the mother hen, must be kept clean. In colder climates (below 20 °C at night), the nest site should be kept warm by lining it with straw and placing it near a stove or fireplace. The chicks should remain with the mother hen for nine to ten weeks, learning from her example how to scavenge and evade predators and other dangers. Clean drinking water and fresh feed in a clean container should be provided to supplement scavenging. See Chapter 3 "Feed Resources" for more detail on feeding techniques.

There is a close relationship between chick weight and growth and mortality rates. In an experiment where young chickens had access to supplementary feed in a creep feeder (Roberts *et al.*, 1994), it was found that supplementary protein feed had a significant effect on the survival rate and growth rate. Chicks separated from the mother hens during the day from the age of three to ten weeks, and fed with chicken starter mash *ad libitum*, had a mortality rate of 20 percent and a body weight of 319 g at ten weeks, compared with a mortality rate of 30 percent and a body weight of 242 g for the control group which remained with the mother hens. See more supplementary detail in the section above, entitled "Creep Feeding". A suitable strategy for rearing chicks therefore would be as follows:

- The chicks should be confined for the first weeks of life and provided with a balanced feed.
- A vaccination programme should be followed.
- Sufficient supplementary feed should be provided during the remaining rearing period to allow the chickens to develop in accordance with their genetic potential.
- Feed supplements and protection should be provided to naturally brooded chickens during the first four to eight weeks of life.

The composition of the supplementary feed will depend on the available scavengable feed, but a form of cafeteria free-choice feeding of a protein concentrate, energy concentrate and calcium mineral in each of three containers may be the best solution.

The mortality rate of naturally brooded chicks, whose only source of feed is from scavenging under free-range conditions, is very high and often exceeds 50 percent up to eight weeks of age. Wickramenratne *et al* (1994) found that predators accounted for up to 88 percent of mortality and that coloured birds had a higher survival rate than white birds. The high mortality rate and the large number of eggs required for hatching are the main causes of low offtake from scavenging poultry flocks. Smith (1990) reported an offtake (sales and consumption) of only 0.3 chickens per hen/year from a survey done on flocks in Nigeria. This low offtake has also been observed in Bangladesh and India.

An efficient way of decreasing mortality rate (a costly loss) is to confine and vaccinate the chicks during the rearing period. This however is more expensive, the cost of feed in particular increasing production costs. A method used over the past ten years in many poultry development projects in Bangladesh confines the chicks during the first eight weeks of life. They are fed approximately 2 kg each of balanced feed and thereafter kept under semi-scavenging conditions. At eight weeks of age, they are less susceptible to attacks by predators and more resistant to diseases, due to their larger body weight and more effective vaccination immunization (due to their better nutrient intake).

## HYGIENE

### *Manure management*

Whatever the type of confinement, proper attention must be paid to manure management. Adult birds produce 500 g of fresh manure (70 percent moisture content) per year per kg of body weight. To preserve its fertilizer value, manure should be dried to about 10 to 12 percent moisture content before storage. This will retain the maximum nitrogen content for fertilizer value. Nitrogen in the form of urea is the most volatile component of manure, and is lost as ammonia if moisture content is too high in the stored material. If the moisture content is too high, then the stored manure releases ammonia, carbon dioxide, hydrogen sulphide and methane, which can have serious physiological effects on humans. Some of these components are also greenhouse gases, which contribute to the global increase in ambient temperature Poultry manure is very useful as an organic fertilizer, as animal and fish feed and as a raw material for methane gas generation in biogas plants for cooking fuel.

### *Other hygiene management measures*

Good ventilation discourages the spread of diseases and pests. In overnight houses, the provision of perches or loosely plaited bamboo mats (such as those used for sieving) placed on the floor can help to keep them dry.

If the birds are housed inside, the floor should be swept daily. An outside chicken house should be cleaned every week to break the breeding cycle of the common housefly. It takes about seven days to complete the breeding cycle from fly egg to hatching of the adult housefly. Wood ash and sand spread on the floor will discourage lice infestation. Mothballs (naphthalene) crushed with ash can also be applied to the feathers or the wings of the birds, or placed where the chickens usually take their dust baths. If the chickens are already infested with mites, the house can be fumigated (while the chickens are outside) with a rag drenched in kerosene. Lice live on the birds, and dust baths with naphthalene powder in the ash will be more effective than dust alone.

The practice of keeping chickens and ducks together should be discouraged. This results in wet floors, giving rise to diseases such as Fowl Cholera. Ducks are also much more tolerant than chickens to Newcastle Disease, and are thus often carriers of this viral disease. Adults and young stock of any poultry should be housed separately to minimize cross-infections and injuries from bullying.

## MANAGEMENT OF FREE-RANGE POULTRY

The unrestricted free-ranging of poultry is often a problem. They trespass onto neighbouring fields and gardens, and are constantly at risk from predators. Confinement is often not practical because of the cost of feed and fencing, while surveillance is only feasible where the very old or very young of the household have time to help. Fencing of vegetable plots is in many cases the best option. Placing more cocks in the village might reduce the movements of the chickens, as the cocks and hens of each flock would keep more to their own territory. Cocks move within an eight-to-ten-house territory, and hens within two or three houses.

Under the free-range system, the difference between the amounts of food gathered through scavenging and the total food requirement for maximum production should be balanced with nutrients supplied from supplementary feed. To make up a properly balanced supplement, it is necessary to know the scavenger feed resource base (SFRB) and the composition of the crop contents (see Chapter 3, SFRB). If this is not known, it is recommended that the fowls have access (using a free-choice cafeteria system) to three containers (or three compartments of a bamboo stem feeder of ingredients comprising a protein concentrate, a carbohydrate source (for energy) and a mineral source (mainly for calcium carbonate for egg shell formation for the hen).

Poultry should have free access to this cafeteria system for two to three hours in the evening to supplement the day's scavenging.

From a feed resource point of view, this recommendation is only economically viable (sustainable) if the consumption of supplementary feed per egg produced is equal to 150 to 180 g or less. Consumption of over 150 g is only justified if the supplements are cheaper than the commercial feed used in intensive poultry production. Supplements are usually recommended in the range of 50 to 80 g/bird/day, so it is usually quite viable. Seasonal variations in the SFRB have a substantial effect on production. During the dry season, scavenged feed from gardens, crops and wasteland (such as grass shoots, seeds, worms, insects and snails) stops, while the quantity and quality of household kitchen waste decrease. The feed supplement should be adjusted seasonally to maintain an optimum level of production or, alternatively, the chicken population could be adjusted to the amount of the SFRB and the feed supplement.

Hens in confinement fed a balanced diet will convert food weight to egg weight at an efficiency of about 2.8 kg of feed per kilogram of egg weight. Changes in husbandry alone may increase the productivity of scavenging village chickens, without the need for additional inputs. In planted orchards, a stocking rate of 120 to 180 birds/ha will clean up windfalls while also fertilizing the trees. In this example, the amount of fertilizer produced per hectare for 150 hens (weighing two kilograms each) is based on the assumption of 500 g of fresh (70 percent moisture) weight of manure produced per kilogram of live weight per year. This results in 330 g of dried manure (dried to a ten percent moisture content) per hen/year, and thus the 150 hens will produce 49.5 kg of dry manure per year. This has an equivalent fertiliser value of 13 percent ammonium nitrate, 8.6 percent super-phosphate and 2.9 percent potash (potassium) salts. Thus the 150 hens will produce the equivalent per hectare/year of 6.4 kg of ammonium nitrate, 4.3 kg of super-phosphate and 1.4 kg of potash salts.

## Planning flock production and size

Production involves birds for meat and eggs. For both meat and egg production, the number of chickens in the flock is the most important factor. Flock size changes constantly as eggs hatch and hens are sold or eaten. Usually the main cause of flock depletion is mortality, particularly in chicks. Disease is the greatest cause of mortality, especially in the rainy season and in the weather changeable humid periods on either side. During summer and the rainy season, predators in the cropped fields also contribute to reduced flock sizes. Local birds lay an average of three to four clutches of 12 to 15 eggs in a year, with more eggs laid at crop harvest time because more feed is available. Given most traditional farming systems, keeping the flock number constant requires eight to ten eggs for reproduction, leaving an average of 35 to 40 eggs per layer for sale or consumption. Because the number of eggs needed for replacement may decrease with better management, the extra eggs can be sold or eaten.

Most egg laying takes place between sunrise to mid-morning. During the months of laying, nest location should not be moved, as this may upset the laying routine.

In village flocks, income derives from the sale of eggs and live birds. For example, a flock of 15 local hens laying 30 eggs/hen/year (with one local cock) will produce 450 eggs in a year. Of these 450 eggs, 120 may be incubated by broody hens (in ten clutches of 12 eggs each), of which 100 chicks may hatch, and 30 eggs may be cracked and consumed in the household, leaving a balance of 300 eggs for sale. Of the 100 day-old chicks, 30 may reach maturity (with rearing losses of 70 percent), to yield 15 cockerels and 15 pullets. The 15 pullets will replace the older hens, of which ten remain after the sale of cull hens, and one new cockerel will replace the old cock. The annual income from the flock can therefore be calculated as follows:

300 eggs + 10 old hens + 1 old cock + 14 cockerels = income

For improved productivity, culling is important and productive birds should be carefully selected. For simplicity, the above example assumes no adult mortality.

# CASE STUDIES OF FAMILY POULTRY MANAGEMENT SYSTEMS

## A free-range system in Ghana

In the traditional free-range system of the Mamprusi tribe in northern Ghana (van Veluw, 1987), the farmer releases his 19 chickens and six guinea fowls from the space under the grain store each morning. Grains are thrown on the ground to feed the birds. A young boy takes care of the birds during the day and protects the crops from poultry damage. Occasionally the boy will feed the birds with a piece of termite hill, and in the evening he returns with the flock and locks them under the granary store.

Chicken hens lay throughout the year, but guinea fowls lay only in the rainy season. Chicken hens produce about 20 to 40 eggs a year and guinea fowls about 50. Most of the eggs are used for hatching. Chickens also hatch guinea fowl eggs, as guinea fowls are not good mothers. Hatching takes place throughout the year, although most of the hens incubate their eggs in the rainy season. A reproduction cycle (laying, hatching, caring for chicks and resting) takes about 20 weeks. Mortality is high (75 percent) among the young chicks. Out of ten chicks, only about two reach adulthood, due mainly to disease, predators and road accidents. Newcastle Disease in particular kills many poultry in the dry season. Worms as internal parasites are a great problem, weakening the birds. Predators include snakes, birds of prey, cats and dogs. Mortality up to two months of age is 50 percent, with a further 25 percent thereafter up to sexual maturity.

Hatchability of guinea fowl eggs is very low (45 percent) compared with chickens (72 percent). Farmers keep hens for about three years and guinea fowls for two years, after which productivity decreases considerably and they are culled.

**Table 4.6** Total annual production of a Mamprusi average flock

| | Chickens | | Guinea fowls | | Total Production |
|---|---|---|---|---|---|
| | Flock | Production | Flock | Production | |
| Cocks | 3 | 1 | 2 | 1 | 2 |
| Hens | 9 | 3 | 4 | 2 | 5 |
| Cockerels | 2 | 22 | - | 13 | 35 |
| Pullets | 5 | 19 | - | 11 | 30 |
| Eggs (/hen) | - | 45 (20) | - | 65 (50) | 110 (380) |

## Scavenging commercial hybrid layers in Sri Lanka

In a study carried out by Roberts and Senaratne (1992), Sri Lankan villagers reared hybrid egg layers in a semi-scavenging system. Day-old hybrid chicks were brooded under the heat of a small kerosene lamp. The chicks were provided with a little mixed supplement of local crop by-products, comprising 40 percent rice polish, 50 percent expeller coconut meal and 10 percent broken rice. The Proximate chemical analysis of this supplement was 16 percent Crude Protein, 8 percent Crude Fat, 7 percent Crude Fibre and 7 percent Ash.

The amount of the supplement increased from 8 to 60 g/bird/day until 12 weeks of age, and was maintained at 60 g thereafter. The growth rate was 38 g/bird/day up to 20 weeks of age. The mortality rate of the chicks was only four percent in the period up to ten weeks, which compared favourably with mortality of 68 percent up to six weeks in Indonesia (Kingston and Creswell, 1982) and 25 percent up to eight weeks in Thailand (Thitisak *et al*, 1989) in chicks hatched and reared by village hens. The comparative advantage of the Sri Lankan performance was attributed to supplementing the competitive scavenging, and to the protection against predators provided by the semi-intensive management system. It is probable that chicks would also benefit from the use of a simple creep feeder for feeding kitchen waste. The mortality rate, in the Sri Lankan example, increased after reaching eight months of age, perhaps due to a greater need for scavenger free-ranging, and almost reached a cumulated 60 percent loss by 13 months of age. Of the 142 hens lost up to 13 months of age, records were kept for 92. The causes of mortality were:

- 32 percent predators (such as dogs, mongooses, pole cats and snakes);
- 26 percent disappeared;
- 15 percent Newcastle disease;
- 15 percent intestinal infection;
- 5 percent stolen;
- 4 percent accidents (vehicles and falling coconuts); and
- 2 percent attacked by humans.

Hens laid their first eggs when they reached 21 weeks (146 days) of age, although 40 percent production (on a hen/day basis) was not achieved until they were 30 weeks of age. Peak egg production was just over 60 percent. A severe drop in production (beginning when the hens were eight months of age) corresponded with an outbreak of Newcastle Disease in local village birds and the start of the long dry intermonsoon period. Production fell to below 30 percent when the hens were ten months of age, and slowly rose again to over 60 percent at 13 months of age. The recovery in production began during the dry period and was maintained into the next season. Egg production was comparable with that of hybrid egg layers, which were introduced into the village as pullets, provided with a supplement and allowed to scavenge.

The production was much better than the 12 to 21 percent reported in village birds in Indonesia (Kingston and Creswell, 1982) and in Thailand (Janviriyasopaki *et al*, 1989) and (Creswell and Gunawane, 1982). The egg weight reported by Roberts and Senaratne (1992) was 60 g compared with about 40 g for village hens (Kingston and Creswell, 1982).

## A free-range system in Senegal

In a study carried out on farms in Senegal (Sall, 1990), flock sizes ranged from under five birds to more than 15 birds, with an average flock size of ten birds. Seven percent of the flocks comprised under five birds, 38 percent comprised five to ten birds, 41 percent comprised 10 to 15 birds, and 14 percent comprised more than 15 birds.

Flocks with fewer than five birds had either recently lost hens or had hens that had not yet hatched their eggs. Flock size varied considerably during the year, due to additions (hatchings, purchases and gifts) and to chickens either sold or lost through disease or predators. The birds were permitted to scavenge during the day and were locked into wooden cages (*ngounou*) at night for protection. The cages were made on the farm from available materials (including bricks, galvanised iron sheets and wood). The doors were small, to prevent entry by thieves and predators. Stock density in the cages was about 25 birds/m$^2$. Feed and water was available to supplement kitchen waste and scavenging.

The proportion of young chicks and growers in the flock was about 60 percent while adults represented 40 percent. Mortality in the first month of age was 40 percent. There were four to five clutches of eggs laid per year, with 8 to 15 eggs per clutch. Egg weights ranged between 38 and 43 g with an average of 40 g. Almost all eggs were set for hatching and of these hatchability was about 80 percent. The production cycle was eight to ten weeks (10 to 15 days for egg laying, 21 days for incubation, and only 34 days for rearing). The chicks remained close to the hens for up to two weeks, during which time there was a relatively low mortality rate of 14 percent. On leaving the immediate protection of the hens, mortality increased sharply to 40 percent between three and four weeks, and up to 66 percent by three months of age. Similarly, the average daily live-weight gain of birds under this extensive system decreased from 10 g at eight weeks to 6 g at 12 weeks.

**Table 4.7** Village flock structure in Senegal Source (Sall, 1990)

| Age (months) | Nº | Males | Nº | Females | Nº | Total % |
|---|---|---|---|---|---|---|
| 0 – 1 | - | - | - | - | 320 | 50.5 |
| 1 – 3 | - | - | - | - | 99 | 15.6 |
| 3 – 6 | 34 | 5.4 | 84 | 13.3 | 118 | 18.6 |
| 6 – 8 | 2 | 0.3 | 21 | 3.3 | 23 | 3.6 |
| 8 -10 | 1 | 0.2 | 19 | 2.9 | 20 | 3.2 |
| 10 + | 15 | 2.4 | 39 | 6.2 | 54 | 8.5 |
| Total | 52 | 8.3 | 163 | 25.6 | 634 | 100 |

**Table 4.8** Age-related mortality in local birds in Senegal

| Age (weeks) | % Mortality (cumulative) |
|---|---|
| 1 | 13 ± 5 |
| 2 | 15 ± 9 |
| 3 | 39 ± 20 |
| 4 | 42 ± 20 |
| 8 | 49± 20 |
| 12 | 66 ± 17 |

Source: Sall, 1990, p 37

**Table 4.9** Body weight of local birds in Senegal

| Age | Nº | Males | Nº | Females | Nº | Males + Females |
|---|---|---|---|---|---|---|
| 1 week | - | - | - | - | 81 | 34±5 |
| 2 weeks | - | - | - | - | 75 | 58±10 |
| 3 weeks | - | - | - | - | 66 | 101±43 |
| 1 month | - | - | - | - | 98 | 171±70 |
| 2 months | - | - | - | - | 41 | 464±242 |
| 3 months | - | - | - | - | 58 | 631±211 |
| 4 months | 29 | 975±20 | 63 | 746±170 | 92 | 860 |
| 6 months | 5 | 1380±150 | 21 | 1229±165 | 26 | 1305 |
| 8 months | 2 | 1826±75 | 21 | 1264±183 | 23 | 1544 |
| 10 months | 1 | 1500 | 19 | 1245±150 | 20 | 1372 |
| + 1 year | 15 | 1803±4 | 39 | 1350±223 | 54 | 1577 |

Source: Sall, 1990

# Chapter 5

# Incubation and Hatching

## NATURAL INCUBATION

The broody hen chosen for natural incubation should be large (to cover and thus keep more eggs warm), healthy and preferably vaccinated, with a good brooding and mothering record. Signs of broodiness are that the hen stops laying, remains sitting on her eggs, ruffles her feathers, spreads her wings and makes a distinctive clucking sound. Brooding may be induced with dummy eggs or even stones.

Eggs usually become fertile about four days after the rooster has been introduced to the hens. A maximum of 14 to 16 eggs may be brooded in one nest, but hatchability often declines with more than ten eggs, depending on the size of the hen. Feed and water provided in close proximity to the hen will keep her in better condition and reduce embryo damage due to the cooling of the eggs if she has to leave the nest to scavenge for food.

The hen keeps the eggs at the correct humidity by splashing water on them from her beak. This is a further reason for providing her with easy access to water. In very dry regions, slightly damp soil can be placed under the nesting material to assist the hen in maintaining the correct humidity (between 60 and 80 percent). Fertile eggs from other birds are best added under the brooding hen between one and four days after the start of brooding. In Bangladesh, it has been reported that local broody hens will even sit on and hatch a second clutch of eggs, often losing considerable weight in the process (especially if insufficient attention is paid to the provision of food and water).

The incubation period for chicken eggs is 20 to 21 days, and increases up to 30 days for other poultry. After sitting for some days, a broody hen can be given some newly hatched chicks and, if they are accepted, the original eggs can be removed and replaced with more chicks. Thus hens with a better record of mothering can be better utilised for their abilities.

Eggs initially need a very controlled heat input to maintain the optimum temperature of 38°C, because the embryo is microscopic in size. As the embryo grows in size (especially after 18 days), it produces more heat than it requires and may even need cooling. Moisture levels of 60 to 80 percent Relative Humidity (increasing during the incubation period) are important to stop excess moisture loss from the egg contents through the porous egg shell and membranes. Factors to consider for successful natural incubation include the following:

- Feed and water should be close to the hen.
- The broody hen should be examined to ensure that she has no external parasites.
- Any eggs stored for incubation should be kept at a temperature between 12 and 14 °C, at a high humidity of between 75 to 85 percent, and stored for no longer than seven days.
- Extra fertile eggs introduced under the hen from elsewhere should be introduced at dusk.
- The eggs should be tested for fertility after one week by holding them up to a bright light (a candling box works best. If there is a dark shape inside the egg (the developing embryo), then it is fertile. A completely clear (translucent) egg is infertile.

A hatchability of 80 percent (of eggs set) from natural incubation is normal, but a range of 75 to 80 percent is considered satisfactory. Setting of hatchings is best timed so that the chicks to be hatched are two months of age at the onset of major weather changes, such as either the rainy (or dry) season or winter/summer. A plentiful natural food supply over the growing period of the chicks will ensure a better chance for their survival. Successful poultry species instinctively lay and incubate their eggs at a time of the year when newly hatched chicks will have a better supply of high protein and energy food provided by the environment. For example, guinea fowl will only lay eggs in the rainy season. However, seasonal changes in weather patterns are also times of greater disease risk.

## ARTIFICIAL INCUBATION (PARCHED PADDY RICE AND RICE HUSK TECHNIQUES)

There are many commercial artificial incubators of varying capacities. Most depend on electricity, but some use gas or kerosene for heating. All use a thermostatic switching device to keep the temperature constant within one Celsius degree. The correct humidity is usually maintained by having a pre-determined surface area of water appropriate for each incubator chamber.

Turning the egg several times each day is important to prevent the embryo from sticking to the shell membranes. With hand-turning systems, an odd number of times turned per day (five to seven times) will ensure that during successive overnight periods the egg is always oriented the opposite way from that of the previous night.

The broody hen carries out all of these incubation tasks instinctively, and artificial incubation attempts to duplicate these tasks. Traditional artificial incubation techniques have evolved over thousands of years in many parts of the world. One such technique, developed for hatching duck eggs in China, is the parched (heated) rice technique. It is based on the use of heated paddy rice and embryo-generated heat. It is still used in China and Bali, Indonesia, with hatchability results of up to 80 percent (Smith, 1990). The objectives of artificial incubation are met equally well using either parched rice or rice husks, and a hatchability of 65 to 75 percent is common. By candling the eggs between days 5 and 7, infertile eggs can be detected as "clears" (as the light is not obscured by the growing embryo). These eggs are still suitable for sale for human consumption, which improves the economic viability of this system.

As duck eggshells are less brittle than chicken eggs, the system was never adopted for chicken eggs in China. The original Chinese system used 80 duck eggs per bundle. However, with extra care, and fewer eggs per bundle (25 to 30 compared with 40 duck eggs), chicken egg incubation was found to be equally successful in Bangladesh when adapted there in the 1980s. The number of duck eggs per bundle was reduced to 40, which gave better hatching results as well as fewer breakages than 80 per bundle.

The artificial parched rice or rice husk incubation process is started by heating the eggs, either in the sun or in an insulated warming room equipped with a heat source. On sunny days, approximately 25 to 30 chicken eggs or 40 duck eggs, (presumed fertile, and carefully dated and labelled) are placed in the sun on pieces of padded cloth for about 30 minutes and turned occasionally to raise the temperature of the eggs to the required 37 to 38 °C. This temperature can be judged by the appearance of water droplets on the shell or by touching the egg to the eyelid. On sunless days, eggs must be placed on a cloth in a shallow bamboo basket and put on racks in a heated warming room to slowly achieve the same temperature. This usually requires approximately one to three hours. Any slow-burning fuel is suitable, and kerosene and charcoal are commonly used. In Egypt, dried beanstalks were used for thousands of years for their characteristic slow-burning property, and are still used today in the Fayoumi district (from where the well-known chicken breed of the same name originates). A well-vented stove will prevent any toxic fumes affecting the embryo. In Bangladesh, slightly heated (to 38°C) sand or wood-ash, covering the eggs for approximately one minute, is also effective in warming the eggs. Human clinical thermometers, now readily available, can be used to assist training in using the eyelid's sensitivity to temperature. If the humidity drops below 70 percent, 60 percent, 50 percent or even 40 percent (particularly in typical progressively drier months), a wet (and slightly warm) cloth should be placed over the eggs with a frequency corresponding to the above humidities of one, two, four or six times daily. This will raise the humidity of the egg so that the embryo will not dry out.

The unhusked (paddy) rice is heated (parched) and continuously stirred until it reaches a temperature of 60°C, to provide heat for the eggs for the first two weeks of incubation. About 2.5 to 3.0 kg of the heated rice is enclosed in a cloth pillow and placed into the egg basket. The pillows have the same diameter (40 cm in the Bangladesh example) as the basket, and should be about 8 cm thick. Where rice-husk is used, pillows can be made with black-coloured material, which easily absorb the sun's heat. When the temperature of the pillow has dropped to about

40°C, a loosely bunched bundle of 40 duck (or 25 to 30 chicken) pre-warmed eggs are placed on top of the warm rice. The bundle is made from a square piece of cloth about 45 cm on each side. A soft duster cloth with pinholes is suitable. Alternating pillows of warm rice and egg bundles are added until the basket is full, finishing with a pillow of rice. The basket is then covered with padding to conserve as much heat as possible. This procedure is repeated until all the eggs are placed in baskets, leaving one basket empty to allow the addition of freshly warmed rice. The incubating baskets are cylindrical in shape (50 cm in diameter and 80 cm in depth in China, and 40 cm in diameter and 70 cm in depth in Bangladesh and are made of woven bamboo strips. In China, a few layers of bamboo paper are pasted on the inner surface of the sides and bottom to seal the gaps against temperature loss through convection.

In warmer parts of southern China, rice husk is substituted for paddy rice, and the pillows containing the husks are made from black-coloured material, which easily heat up in the sun. Rice husks also provide very good insulation against loss of heat from the older eggs, which is instead transferred (by conduction) to younger eggs placed in contact with them in separate bundles. This rice-husk system was adopted on a large scale in Bangladesh after being introduced by poultry development projects in the 1980s. The system has evolved, and the cylindrical egg baskets are now set into larger bamboo frame setting boxes, with more insulating rice husk material placed between the cylinders and the walls of the enclosing setting boxes. The cylinder wall should be about 10 cm from the setting box wall and 8 cm from the next cylinder. With this greater insulation, there is less heat loss, thus less need to provide supplementary heat from costly fuels.

For the first three days, reheated paddy rice (or rice husk) is added three times a day at regular intervals. During days four to six, this may be reduced to twice a day. The object is to ensure that the eggs are kept at the temperature most suitable for embryo development. The spare basket is used to transfer eggs from an adjoining basket when adding freshly warmed rice or rice-husks. Thus the top layer of eggs becomes the bottom layer and the bottom layer ends up on top of the spare cylinder. The newly emptied basket is then ready to receive eggs from the third basket, and so the cycle continues.

In China, heat is provided for days 13 to 14 in summer and in the colder months also on days 18 to 19. After that, the developing embryos are able to produce enough heat to maintain the incubation process without further need of an outside heat source. Eggs set for the first six days are called "new eggs", those between days 6 to 13 (which neither need nor produce extra heat) are "in-between eggs" and eggs after day 13 (which give out excess heat) are "old eggs". Once a basket contains "old" and "in-between eggs", it is possible to use embryo-generated heat alone to incubate "new eggs", which are usually introduced at intervals into the basket and placed between layers of "old eggs". Even when outside heat is not added, the eggs in the baskets must be regularly turned and aired three to five times a day in the process of transferring them to adjoining baskets. In order to use the embryo-generated heat effectively (almost all year round), the layers of eggs in the baskets are organized to a particular pattern, a typical example of which is shown in Table 5.1.

The eggs are candled on days 5 and 13, both to identify infertile eggs and dead embryos and to assess the degree of embryo development; which is used as one of the guides in adjusting basket temperature. Placing the egg on the upper eyelid allows the egg temperature to be assessed. The temperature of the basket may be adjusted in the following ways:

- by varying the proportion of eggs in a basket at different stages of incubation (for example, the temperature may be lowered by removing some of the bundles of "old eggs");
- by varying the arrangement of eggs in a basket (for example, as heat dissipation from eggs near the sides of the basket is faster than from those in the centre; a bundle of "old eggs" can be placed in the centre core and bundles of "new eggs" shaped to enclose them); and

- by changing the top covering of the basket using heavier padded material in cold weather and at the beginning of the incubation period, and a lighter covering if less heat retention is required.

**Table 5.1** Arrangement of eggs in the incubation baskets prior to and after transfer to adjoining baskets

| Layer | Before transfer | Incubation time (days) Summer | Winter | After transfer |
|---|---|---|---|---|
| 1 | A | 14-6 | 17-20 | J |
| 2 | B | 1-3 | 1-4 | I |
| 3 | C | 10-13 | 13-16 | H |
| 4 | D | 4-6 | 5-8 | G |
| 5 | E | 7-9 | 9-12 | F |
| 6 | F | 7-9 | 9-12 | E |
| 7 | G | 4-6 | 5-8 | D |
| 8 | H | 10-13 | 13-16 | C |
| 9 | I | 1-3 | 1-4 | B |
| 10 | J | 14-16 | 17-20 | A |

Source: Fuan, 1987

Eggs in the advanced stages of incubation produce a lot of heat, so on days 13 to 14 in summer (days 18 to 19 in winter), the "old eggs" are transferred to hatching beds, where they are placed in a single layer for final development and hatching. The surface of the bed is covered with a thin layer of rice husks and then covered with a straw mat. The edges of the bed are lined with padding to protect the eggs. The covering for the developing eggs in the bed may be heavy or light cloth, depending on the degree of insulation required. The temperature in the hatching bed is maintained at 36 to 37 °C, slightly lower than that of the basket. The temperature can be adjusted by changing the thickness of the covering, varying the space between the eggs, and moving the eggs twice a day so that those on the perimeter change places with those at the centre. In very hot dry weather, the eggs are sprayed with a fine mist of water. They are kept in the bed until the chicks hatch out and dry.

The hatching bed should be two-storied (like a bed-bunk) and can be made of wood. An example hatching bed with a 500-egg capacity has a length of 90 cm and width of 68 cm. The height of the side wall on all sides should be 20 cm from the bed base level, with a 25 cm gap above the side wall for ventilation and ease of access.

# Chapter 6
# Health

In most family flocks, disease is an important problem. Although farmers are familiar with the signs and symptoms of disease (see Table 6.1), the underlying causes are less well known. Almost every farmer and most extension workers hold Newcastle Disease (ND) responsible for most deaths, and the disease has a local name in all languages.

**Table 6.1** Signs of poultry disease observed by farmers in East Kalimantan villages, Indonesia

| **Signs** | **Frequency %** |
|---|---|
| Chickens huddle together | 16.1 |
| Coughing, sneezing, rapid breathing | 13.2 |
| Discharge from mouth and nostrils | 10.9 |
| Dullness, no appetite, closed eyes | 10.9 |
| Paralysis of legs and wings | 9.2 |
| White droppings | 8.6 |
| Turned or twisted neck | 8.0 |
| Dark red colour of head and comb | 6.9 |
| Greenish or yellow droppings | 4.6 |
| Bloody reddish droppings | 4.0 |
| Swellings of head and comb | 2.9 |
| Pale comb | 1.7 |
| Worms in faeces | 1.7 |
| Eye worm | 1.1 |

Source: Ramm *et al.*, 1984

However, not all infectious diseases are due to the Newcastle Disease Virus (NDV). Digestive problems resulting in slow growth and diarrhoea may be the result of rancid feed or too much salt, and may also be symptoms of diseases such as coccidiosis, salmonellosis, or Gumboro Disease (Also called Infectious Bursal Disease [IBD]). ND often has the symptom of greenish faeces, which indicates a loss of appetite.

Poultry have highly developed and sophisticated respiratory systems. Their heart and breathing rate are faster than humans, and their body temperature is 5 °C higher. Their lungs are connected at the lower ends to a complex series of membrane-enclosed air sacs, which in turn are connected to air cavities in their major skeletal bones. These features contribute to their lightness and flying ability. The disadvantage is extreme susceptibility to respiratory infections caused by a wide range of bacteria, viruses and fungi. These infections become more of a problem in domestication, which usually involves some degree of increase in stock density – even if only for overnight accommodation – and thus increases the risk of cross-infection.

Inadequate ventilation of poultry houses results in a build-up of ammonia gas from poultry faeces, which contain urea. This can predispose the poultry to respiratory disorders, such as sneezing, running eyes and mucous discharges from the mouth. Providing good ventilation easily prevents this. More prolonged respiratory disorders are usually caused by diseases such as ND, Infectious Bronchitis (IB), Infectious Laryngotracheitis (ILT), Chronic Respiratory Disease (CRD) and diphtheria.

Coordination disorders such as paralysis, limping, twisted neck and slow movement may be caused by a variety of factors, such as physical injury, nutrient deficiencies and diseases, including ND (twisted necks or *torticolis*), Marek's Disease (paralysis), synovitis (tendon infections in which feet joints feel warm) and Avian Encephalomyelitis (AE).

## COMMON DISEASES

The common diseases and disorders of free-range poultry may be either infectious or non-infectious, and are caused by a wide range of organisms or deficiencies. These are summarised in Table 6.2. Disease control is discussed in a later section of this chapter.

**Table 6.2** Causes and examples of poultry diseases

| Causal Agent | Example |
|---|---|
| **Infectious** | |
| Virus | Newcastle Disease, Avian Encephalomyelitis, |
| | Fowl Pox, Marek's Disease, Infectious Bronchitis |
| | Infectious Laryngotracheitis, Gumboro Disease (Infectious Bursal Disease), Duck Virus Hepatitis |
| Mycoplasma | Chronic Respiratory Disease |
| Bacteria | Fowl Cholera, Salmonellosis, Pullorum, Fowl Typhoid, Infectious Sinusitis, Colibacilosis |
| Parasites | **Ectoparasites**: lice, mites, ticks |
| | **Endoparasites**: nematodes, Histomoniasis, Haemoparasites, round worms, hair worms, Avian Malaria |
| | **Protozoa**: Coccidiosis, Blackhead |
| Fungus | Aspergillosis: *A. flavis* (toxins), *A. fumigatus* (airsaculitis) |
| **Non-Infectious** | |
| Deficiencies | rickets, curled toe paralysis, encephalomalacia |
| Toxicities | salt poisoning, food poisoning (Botulism *Clostridium botulinum* and *C. perfringens*), poisonous plants |

## INFECTIOUS DISEASES

### Viral diseases

Viral diseases are some of the most important infectious diseases affecting poultry. They are characterised by not being able to be treated, but most can be prevented with vaccines. The more important viral diseases are outlined below.

#### *Newcastle Disease (ND)*

This disease (called Ranikhet Disease in Asia) spreads rapidly via airborne droplets spread by the coughing or sneezing of infected birds. The virus can be carried by wild birds, through contaminated eggs, and on clothing. As mortality is often 100 percent in young chickens, ND is probably the most important constraint to family poultry development. Birds of any age can be affected, although young ones are more susceptible. Mortality in older chickens is usually lower, but egg production is usually severely reduced.

The incubation period of three to five days is followed by dullness, coughing, sneezing and gasping. Rapid breathing is accompanied by a gurgling noise in the throat. The respiratory signs usually develop first and are sometimes followed by nervous signs, characterized by twisting of the neck, sometimes combined with dragging of wings and legs. Depending on the environment and the degree of resistance of the birds, not all symptoms may be shown, or they may be in a mild or subclinical form. Some farmers have observed that the twisting of the neck occurs only in birds that survive. Early loss of appetite results in a greenish diarrhoea. The most obvious diagnostic sign of ND is very sudden, very high mortality, often with few symptoms having had time to develop. Diagnosis of ND can be difficult from just the symptoms, as they are so varied, and as many other diseases share the same symptoms. For a discussion on the control of ND, see the "ND Control" section below. The high incidence of ND among family free-range flocks is due to the following factors:

- the prevalence of virulent strains (velogenic, viscerotropic and pneumotropic) in tropical countries;
- continuous contact with other domestic and wild species of birds (such as ducks and pigeons), which can carry the virus without showing the disease (Majiyagbe and Nawathe, 1981); and
- uncontrolled movement of birds between villages.

There is a seasonal pattern to outbreaks of ND (Sharma *et al.*, 1986), influenced by:

- the arrival of migratory birds;
- changes in climatic conditions leading to stress, which predisposes birds to the disease;
- hot, dry and windy periods, which encourage airborne spread of the virus; and
- overuse of the few supply points of water available (during the dry season), which then become heavily contaminated with the virus.

***Fowl pox***

Fowl pox is still prevalent in many poultry flocks, for the following reasons:

- The fowl pox virus can remain alive in the pox scabs (which have fallen off the birds) for up to ten years, which contaminate the environment.
- Mosquitoes and other blood-sucking insects can transmit the virus.

The disease tends to be seasonal, occurring after mosquito breeding times. It is endemic in Papua New Guinea, where it is significant economically because the only NDV in the country is the non-symptomatic form (Sugrim, 1987). It is also a major disease in many other tropical countries.

***Marek's Disease***

Infection occurs early in life, and once a bird is infected, it can shed the virus in skin flakes throughout its life, if it survives. Clinical signs occur in young growing birds in the Acute Marek's Disease (MD) form, characterised by high mortality from visceral tumours. Another peak of mortality occurs in the Classical MD form, characterized by nerve paralysis in the legs and wings of birds aged from 15 weeks to early in the laying period.

## Mycoplasmal diseases

Mycoplasmas are not classified as bacteria or viruses, but as Pleuro-pneumonia-cocci-like organisms (PPLO). These are primarily associated with Chronic Respiratory Disease (CRD), a complex syndrome caused by *Mycoplasma gallisepticum* in partnership with bacteria (often *E. coli*), fungi and viruses (often Infectious Bronchitis). *M. gallisepticum* can be transmitted through the egg. Multi-age flocks, nutritional deficiency and water deprivation are important factors in the epidemiology of the disease in rural poultry flocks.

## Bacterial diseases

### *Fowl Cholera (Avian Pasteurellosis)*

This is a contagious septicaemia (caused by *Pasteurella multocida*) that affects all types of fowls. It is often transmitted by wild birds or other domestic birds, and spreads by contamination of the feed or water and by oral or nasal discharges from infected birds. The incubation period is four to nine days, but acute outbreaks can occur within two days of infection. In some cases, birds die within a few hours of showing the first signs, which vary depending on the form of the disease. The respiratory form is characterized by gasping, coughing and sneezing, while in the septicaemic form there is diarrhoea with wet grey, yellow, or green droppings. In the localized form, the signs are lameness and swelling of legs or wing joints. In acute cases, the head and comb change colour to dark red or purple. If the infection is localized in the region of the ears, a twisted neck (*torticolis*) can sometimes be observed. In chronic cases, the comb is usually pale, with swellings around the eyes and a discharge from the beak or nostril. Fowl Cholera is common everywhere among free-range village flocks, because they are comprised of different species and are in continuous contact with wild birds.

### *Pullorum (Bacillary White Diarrhoea)*

This is an egg-transmitted disease (caused by *Salmonella pullorum*) that spreads during incubation or just after hatching. White diarrhoea can be seen from three days to several weeks of age. The chicks refuse to eat, keep their heads tucked in and their wings hanging down. They huddle together and make a peeping sound. Mortality in the acute form ranges from 20 to 80 percent, and in the chronic form is around five percent. In the chronic form, the signs are a marked swelling of the hock joints, poor feather development, lack of appetite and depression. Table 6.3 shows the results of a survey in Zaria, Nigeria, conducted by Adesiyun *et al.* (1984) for Pullorum antibodies, which indicate a past infection with the bacteria.

**Table 6.3** Prevalence of *Salmonella pullorum* antibody in chickens in northern Nigeria

| Management | Age (wks) | N° tested | N° positive | (%) |
|---|---|---|---|---|
| Free-range | young | 59 | 15 | 25 |
| (indigenous) | adult | 101 | 40 | 40 |
| Backyard | young | 90 | 8 | 9 |
| (exotic) | 20 + | 70 | 24 | 34 |
| Confinement | young | 70 | 22 | 31 |
| (exotic) | 20 + | 90 | 69 | 77 |

Source: Adesiyun *et al.*, 1984

The free-range stock sampled was indigenous, and the other two groups were exotic. As the age of the birds in the free-range survey was not known, birds not in lay were counted as young.

### *Fowl Typhoid*

Fowl typhoid is caused by *Salmonella gallinarum*, and commonly affects adult fowls. When it occurs in young birds, the signs are similar to those of *S. pullorum*. The incubation period is four to five days, and two days later the birds become depressed and anorexic. The colour of the comb and wattles becomes dark red; the droppings become yellow and the birds close their eyes and keep their heads down. Usually the affected chickens die within three to six days. Pullorum and fowl typhoid complex are both prevalent under free-range conditions.

### *Avian Salmonellosis (Paratyphoid)*

Salmonellosis is usually used to describe infection with any organism of the Salmonella group other than *S. pullorum* or *S. gallinarium*. In countries with intensive poultry systems, poultry meat and eggs are a major source of infection for humans. The opposite may be true of family poultry, with humans infecting poultry. Ojeniyi (1984) reported that *S. hirschfeldii* was isolated from cloacal swab samples in fowls and from an adult human male in the same village.

## Parasitic diseases

### *External parasites (ectoparasites)*

These are very common in scavenging poultry, and include:

- **Lice**: these live on the skin of the birds, especially around the cloacae and under the wings. The irritation they cause can lead to reduced production. Lice species commonly found on poultry are *Menacanthus straminens, Lipeurus caponis, Monopon gallinae, Goniodes gigas* and *Chelopistes meleagride.*
- **Mites**: these are troublesome ectoparasites, which hide in the cracks of housing and perches, and come out only at night. They are bloodsuckers and lower egg production. Mites such as *Dermanyssus gallinae* can also transmit the bacteria *Borrelia,* which causes fever, depression, cyanosis and anaemia (spirochaetosis).
- **Ticks**: a heavy infestation can produce severe anaemia and, in extreme cases, death due to blood loss. *Argas persicus* is particularly dangerous, being the vector of several blood parasites such as the haemoprotozoa and microfilaria. In Malaysia, it was reported (Sani *et al.*, 1987) that out of 201 blood samples taken from village birds, more than 100 contained *Leucocytozoon sabrazesi*, 30 had microfilaria, and six carried *Plasmodium gallinaceum* (Avian malaria). Avian malaria infection is much higher among exotics and cross-breeds.

### *Internal parasites (endoparasites)*

The more important internal parasites are:

- Helminths (worms): these are common in scavenging poultry, especially nematodes and cestodes. Ssenyonga (1982) showed that worms were a major cause of lowered egg production of scavenging poultry in Uganda, the most commonly found being *Ascaridia galli* (Round Worm), *Heterakis gallinae* (Caecal Worm), *Syngamus trachae* (Tracheal Worm) and *Raillientina* spp. (Tape Worm).
- Protozoa: the most pathogenic are the coccidiosis disease species of *Eimeria tenella* and *E. necatrix*. Coccidiosis is a common parasitic infection in scavenging poultry. It affects mostly young birds, and the most important signs are emaciation, thirst, listlessness, ruffled plumage, bloodstained faeces and birds huddling together. Surveys in Southeast Asia and East Africa showed that 73 and 47 percent of birds, respectively, had positive faecal samples of *Eimeria* spp. (Eissa, 1987). The presence of the coccidia organism in faecal samples indicates an infection, but not necessarily at clinical disease levels. Like antibody presence in blood samples, it may indicate a degree of immunity. This should not be "treated", as doing so eliminates the immunity.

## Fungal diseases

### *Mycotoxicosis*

The fungus *Aspergillus flavus* commonly grows on stored feed ingredients where moisture content is over eleven percent, especially cereal grains (such as maize [corn]) and oilcake meal (such as groundnut [peanut] meal). The aflatoxin called mycotoxin is the specific toxin produced by *A. flavus.* The toxin itself may remain after all sign of the fungus mould is gone. Ducks are more vulnerable to the toxin (with a lethal dose in the feed of one part per million [ppm] of aflatoxin) than chicken, which can tolerate up to four ppm. In acute forms of the disease, mortality can be as high as 50 percent. Common adverse effects include immunosuppression, reduced growth in young stock and reduced egg production in hens (Smith, 1990).

***Aspergillosis***

This disease is also called airsaculitis. The fungus *Aspergillus fumigatus* causes the disease by growing as a fungus in the lungs and interconnected air sacs. The fungus grows on damp litter or feed, and the bird breathes in the spores, which grow into easily visible lesions as green and yellow nodules, which can completely fill the lungs.

## NON-INFECTIOUS DISEASES

### Deficiencies

Poultry health is also affected by nutritional and environmental factors, such as insufficient feed or feed deficiencies. A high mortality rate among chicks during the first days or weeks after hatching may be caused by insufficient feed and water. A high mortality in adult birds may be due to nutritional problems, such as salt deficiency.

Energy and protein deficiencies and imbalances can arise when the feed contains insufficient quantities of these nutrients, resulting in poor growth in young stock and a drop in egg production and egg weight in laying hens. Mineral and vitamin deficiencies may result in poor growth, low production or death. Vitamin D deficiency causes rickets (bone deformities) in young chicks and, if combined with a calcium deficiency, in chickens of all ages. A lack of manganese results in deformities of the feet of older chickens.

### Toxicities

An excess of certain nutrients, especially minerals, can cause abnormalities. An excess of common salt (NaCl), for example, results in deformed eggshells as well as increased water consumption, and if drinking water is restricted (as is often the case with free-ranging birds), signs of toxicity may develop. Free access to feed of high carbohydrate and low fat, combined with lack of exercise, high temperatures and stress, can cause Fatty Liver Syndrome, which can result in high mortality.

Ingestion of toxic plant parts (such as leaves, seeds and sap) is a common hazard for free-range birds. Some toxins are produced by micro-organisms, such as those liberated by the bacteria *Clostridium botulinum* and *C. perfringens*, both found in the soil. *C. perfringens* causes necrotic enteritis, caused when the bacteria multiplies in the favourable conditions of the digestive tract and liberates a potent toxin that results in high mortality. Occasionally affected birds show anorexia, depression and diarrhoea, but most die without showing any clinical signs. *C. botulinum* causes botulism disease, which is acute food poisoning. This is more common in ducks, which show the nervous symptoms of neck bent down and feathers falling out easily when lightly pulled. Botulism results from the bird eating rotting vegetable scraps, which contain the toxins produced by the *C. botulinum*. Household vegetable scraps which are not regularly removed are a potential hazard for botulism.

## EPIDEMIOLOGY

### Management system effects

Although nearly all the important poultry diseases are found under all types of management, the pattern of disease in free-range birds is different from that seen in intensive poultry production. Free-range flocks usually comprise different species of all ages, and are constantly exposed to the weather, environment and seasonal outbreaks of disease, as well as to germs and parasites found in the soil and in wild birds and animals.

In a 15-year study of the incidence of poultry diseases in northern Nigeria, Sa'idu *et al.* (1994) found viral infections (such as ND in chickens and pox in turkeys) to be the most common cause of disease, although concurrent viral infection with parasites constituted about half the cases studied (see Table 6.3). They concluded that viruses and parasites caused the most important diseases in indigenous chickens and that they were seasonal in their onset.

Table 6.4 Diseases affecting local chickens and turkeys in Zaria, northern Nigeria

| **Chickens** | |
|---|---|
| **Disease** | **Proportionate mortality (%)** |
| Newcastle Disease | 36.1 |
| COMBINATIONS | 28.5 |
| Snake bite | 8.6 |
| Other Diseases | 8.6 |
| Gumboro | 7.1 |
| Fowl Pox | 5.1 |
| Ectoparasites | 3.5 |
| Endoparasites | 2.5 |
| **Turkeys** | |
| **Disease** | **Proportion of all diseases (%)** |
| Turkey pox | 16.5 |
| Ectoparasites | 15.7 |
| Newcastle Disease | 12.2 |
| COMBINATIONS | 10.6 |
| Infectious sinusitis | 10.2 |
| Endoparasites | 3.5 |
| Other Diseases | 31.3 |

Source: Sa'idu *et al.*, 1994

Another study (Adene and Ayandokun, 1992), which looked at the changing pattern of diseases in southern Nigeria over the period from 1949 to 1955, found that mortality in the free-ranging flocks at the University of Ibadan was due mostly to the following:

- Helminthiasis, due to *Raillietina, Heterakis, Ascaridia, Capillaria, Tetrameres* and *Syngamus* spp.;
- Pediculosis, due to *Menopon, Gonoeodes, Goniocotes and Lipeuris* spp.; and tropical poultry mites (*Ornithonyssus bursa*) in chickens, and *Numidilipueria tropicalis* in guinea fowls.

These parasitic infections were greater causes of mortality than Newcastle Disease at that time.

Another survey of backyard chicken flocks in Zimbabwe (Kelly *et al.*, 1994) tested 450 blood samples from 52 flocks, and found Infectious Bronchitis (IB) in 85 percent and Newcastle Disease (ND) in only 27 percent of the samples (see Table 6.4). A possible explanation for the lower frequency of ND is that the mortality is usually much higher from ND than for IB, so fewer birds survive to be counted.

Similarly, in Zambia, a survey based on 2000 blood samples (Alders *et al.*, 1994) found that the mean seroprevalence of Newcastle Disease was 37 percent, which varied between 29 percent in the northern province and 51 percent in the Copper-belt province. A summary of the relative importance of poultry diseases gathered from other sources is tabulated in Table 6.5.

**Table 6.5** Disease status in backyard chicken flocks in Zimbabwe as shown by blood testing

| Pathogens | Percent positive samples |
|---|---|
| Infectious Bronchitis | 85 |
| Reticulo-endotheliosis | 65 |
| Gumboro Disease | 55 |
| *Pasteurella multocida* | 52 |
| *Mycoplasma gallisepticum* and /or *Mycoplasma synoviae* | 33 |
| Newcastle Disease | 27 |
| Encephalomyelitis | 11 |
| Avian Leucosis | 9 |
| Reovirus | 3 |

Source: Kelly et al., 1994

**Table 6.6** Relative importance of family poultry diseases

| Rank | Saunders 1984 Burkina Faso | Adene 1990 Nigeria | Ramm *et al.,* 1984 Indonesia | Ahmed 1987 Bangladesh |
|---|---|---|---|---|
| 1 | ND | ND | ND | ND |
| 2 | Trichomonas | Gumboro | CRD | Fowl Cholera |
| 3 | Fowl Pox | Fowl Pox | Fowl Pox | Coccidiosis |
| 4 | Salmonellosis | F. typhoid | Coccidiosis | Fowl pox |
| 5 | Pasteurellosis | Marek's Disease | Fowl Cholera | Pullorum |
| 6 | Parasites | Parasites | Pullorum | Parasites |

## Poultry species effects

In tropical countries, Newcastle Disease is considered to be the most important disease of village flocks because of its high mortality, which is above 70 percent in most African countries. However, not all poultry species are equally susceptible. Guinea fowl, although sometimes affected, appear to have better resistance to ND even when kept with chickens. They are however more susceptible to *Trichomonas,* to which chickens appear to be immune. Ducks are not thought to be susceptible to ND (although they are significant carriers of the disease), or to most other common diseases of chicken, but they succumb easily to diseases specific to ducks, such as:

- Duck Virus Enteritis (Duck Plague): this is an acute and highly contagious disease of ducks, with a mortality rate of up to 100 percent.
- Duck Virus Hepatitis and Mycotoxicosis: these pose a great danger for ducklings. Mycotoxicosis is mostly contracted from ingesting aflatoxin from mouldy compound feeds; a dose of 0.75 ppm can kill a duckling.
- Duck Cholera (*Pasteurella multocida* infection): this is a widespread disease of ducklings in village flocks, and chickens can also be infected.
- Pasteurellosis (*Pasteurella anapestifer*): this is an important disease of ducklings, while *Escherichia coli* infection (Colibacillosis) is a septicaemic disease of growing ducks. Chickens can also be infected with *E. coli*.

The above diseases are largely responsible for the huge losses of ducklings that are a feature of free-range duck production.

Although salmonellosis is not a major disease in ducks, duck eggs are a significant source of salmonellosis in humans. This may explain the taboo against touching duck eggs prevalent in many cultures, particularly in Africa. Duck eggs should not be stored in contact with vegetables that will be eaten raw, such as carrots, lettuce and cabbage.

## Season and age effects

Disease patterns vary according to the season. Newcastle Disease is more serious during the dry season. In Thailand, Pasteurellosis, Coryza and streptococcal infections also occur more frequently in the dry season, and Fowl Cholera, Colibacillosis and Pseudomoniasis in the rainy season (Thitisak, 1992). In northern Nigeria, where Sa'idu *et al.* (1994) studied 522 cases involving 8 800 chickens, ND accounted for 30 percent of all cases. Of these, 38 percent occurred immediately before the dry season of October to December, and only 10 percent during the rainy season of July to September. As for Fowl Pox, more outbreaks occurred in the rainy season and were highest in the month of July, and about 60 percent of the outbreaks affected young chicks. In Thailand, Thitisak *et al.* (1989) noted that a catastrophic mortality had occurred in March in both 1987 and 1988, this being the late dry season when early storms cause sudden drops in temperature which chill the birds. They also found that chickens under two months of age (normally a rapid growth-rate phase), and those over six months of age (in the process of becoming sexually mature) were more susceptible to infectious diseases (see Table 6.6).

**Table 6.7** Cause-specific mortality rates per 100 birds at risk

| **Cause of death** | **Age (months)** | | | |
|---|---|---|---|---|
| | **under 2** | **2 to 6** | **Over 6** | **Total** |
| Infectious Coryza | 6.8 | 0.7 | 16.8 | 24.3 |
| Avian Pasteurellosis | 4.6 | 1.1 | 2.4 | 8.1 |
| Newcastle Disease | 4.1 | 1.4 | 0.7 | 6.2 |
| Fowl Pox | 3.2 | 0.3 | 0.0 | 3.5 |
| Salmonellosis | 1.4 | 0.0 | 0.3 | 1.7 |
| Pseudomonas | 0.0 | 0.3 | 0.0 | 0.3 |
| **Total** | **20.0** | **3.8** | **20.2** | **44.1** |

Source: Thitisak *et al.*, 1989, and Janviriyasopak *et al.*, 1989.

Data from surveys in 1987 of 2231 and 3239 birds

## Need for epidemiological studies

Epidemiological studies of village poultry are essential for the development of appropriate village-based poultry health programmes. These have been attempted in many countries, but the work undertaken in Thailand (Janviriyasopa *et al.*, 1989) will be used as an example.

The North-Eastern Regional Veterinary Research and Diagnostic Centre, Tha Pra, Khon Kaen, Thailand, with assistance from the German Agency for Technical Cooperation (GTZ) and the Department of Veterinary Clinical Sciences of Massey University, New Zealand, embarked on a long term-study ("Health and Productivity of Native Chickens"). This was part of a programme of epidemiological investigations of factors affecting livestock productivity in the region. The objective of the study was to decide on the priority of the problems for which control programmes could be developed within the regional Basic Poultry Health Service.

In selected villages, about 15 families with flocks of 15 to 20 birds were recruited. In most of the villages, vaccinations against ND, Fowl Pox and Fowl Cholera were carried out in order to encourage interest. Two villages were paid to represent a totally unvaccinated control population. Birds were wing-tagged and grouped by age:

- under two months;
- two to six months;
- six to twelve months;
- one to two years;
- two to three years; and
- over three years of age.

During each visit, the number of eggs and chickens were weighed, counted and scored, and blood was collected from the wing vein for determination of ND titre and for Pullorum, CRD, IB and Gumboro (IBD) tests. Each tagged bird was subjected to health, feather and ectoparasite scoring. Sick and dead birds were collected for pathological examinations at the laboratory, in order to identify the cause of death or illness, and refrigerators were provided in some villages to store dead birds for later examination. Dead or diseased birds were exchanged for healthy birds in order to examine as many as possible, but as the villagers would sometimes eat dead or dying birds, most of those exchanged tended to be the immature birds which owners were less willing to eat. By calculating age-specific mortality rates and then determining cause-specific rates within each age-group, the contribution of each disease to the mortality within an age-group was determined. A questionnaire was used to gather additional information.

The objectives of the survey were to establish:

- a productivity index;
- population dynamics;
- the importance of common diseases, their incidence and prevalence;
- the average life span of birds;
- patterns of disease outbreaks; and
- the relationship between disease and production levels.

The parameters used for the survey were:

- egg production;
- egg hatching rate;
- number of deaths in each age group;
- weight gain of growers;
- number of birds killed for eating;
- number of birds sold; and
- unexpected losses.

Some of the results of the survey are seen in Table 6.6 above. Poor management of eggs, hatching and young chicks, as well as malnutrition, particularly in the dry season, were found to be important predisposing factors to infectious diseases and parasitic infestation (Thitisak *et al.*, 1989).

## DISEASE CONTROL IN FAMILY FLOCKS

### Non-medical disease control

The most economical and effective means of preventing non-viral diseases is improved management and nutrition, of which the most important aspects are hygiene, housing, flock structure, and young chick care and feeding.

#### *Hygiene*

The following simple hygiene measures, which help in disease prevention, were recommended by the FAO/UNDP Small Stock Development Project in North Kivu, Zaire (FAO/Anonymous, 1989):

- Droppings, feathers and dead birds are sources of pathogens and should be removed from overnight housing and the free-range compound, and then properly disposed of. This will also reduce the incidence of external parasites.
- New arrivals to the flock should be isolated. Birds bought or received as gifts should be quarantined in a basket or cage for at least 15 days; if they remain healthy, they can then join the flock.
- All new arrivals should be treated for ectoparasites and endoparasites as well as vaccinated on arrival if possible.
- Sick birds should be isolated or slaughtered promptly, and dead birds buried.
- The litter in the poultry house should be turned frequently and changed if wet.
- Overnight security baskets should be put in the sun to dry properly or suspended near a fire during the rainy season.
- Feeders and drinkers should be cleaned frequently.
- Broken pots used as drinkers should be heated over a fire before refilling.
- The poultry house or basket should be regularly disinfected every two months.

#### *Housing*

Simple improvements and maintenance can be carried out when the poultry house is not in use. Important factors in good housing are:

- **Ventilation**: if poultry baskets are used for overnight housing, they should not be covered with cloths or sacks. Huts, coops and baskets should not be placed near dunghills or pit latrines.
- **Proper spacing**: overcrowding should be avoided, and numbers of poultry should be restricted to the space available. Weaned chicks and growers should be kept in separate overnight housing. Laying and brooding nests should be left undisturbed.
- **Separate species**: it is better to keep only one species of poultry but if this is not possible, the species should be housed separately overnight to avoid the spread of disease.

#### *Flock structure*

Of all the common free-range poultry species, chickens are the most susceptible to disease. Ducks, geese and guinea fowl are often symptom-less carriers of chicken diseases, or have mild forms of them. This represents a common source of infection in chickens, while the opposite is rare. Therefore in mixed flocks special attention should be paid to the health of chickens. Separation into different species and age groups may not be possible, but simple devices such as creep cage-baskets may be used as a temporary measure for procedures such as vaccination of chicks or special feeding.

### *Feeding*

The importance of nutrition in flock health is well known. There is a need for further research into alternative feeds for rural poultry, which avoid the use of grain for human consumption (see Chapter 3).

## Medical disease control

Simple medical control measures appropriate for free-range village flocks include:

- Vaccination against Newcastle Disease, Fowl Pox and Fowl Cholera.
- Deworming for internal parasites in a mixed flock, with a polyvalent poultry dewormer such as Piperazine (added to drinking water). With guinea fowl, a dewormer against *Trichomonas* should be used.
- Treatment for external parasites. Insects and other external parasites build up quickly in poultry huts, coops and baskets. There are effective traditional methods against ectoparasites. All the surfaces of the basket, coop or hut can be sprayed with a suitable insecticide, using the same type of hand-pump used for spraying mosquitoes. This procedure should only be carried out when the house is empty in the morning, and the birds should not be allowed back inside until evening. External parasites living on poultry can best be treated by adding powdered mothballs (naphthalene) and ash to the dust bath area. Ash dust is more abrasive than ordinary soil dust, and thus removes the waxy coating of the insect exoskeleton when the bird takes a dust bath. If enough of the waxy coating is removed, the insect will dehydrate and die.

## Newcastle Disease control

There are three general approaches to the control of ND:

- **Hygiene:** this is always important, especially in the control of ND in semi-intensive systems where birds are confined within a fenced yard or house. Hygiene includes measures such as cleaning, disinfection, limiting access to wild birds, and personal hygiene of the farm staff.
- **Slaughter of infected flocks**: this is a drastic measure, which has been successfully employed in isolated regions or islands that are essentially free of the disease.
- **Vaccination** in combination with appropriate hygiene measures: this remains the most effective way of controlling ND.

### *Newcastle Disease vaccines and vaccination campaigns*

For viral diseases, vaccination is the only form of prevention. A proper vaccination campaign can rapidly and significantly minimize losses due to disease. In Indonesia, after an ND vaccination campaign, mortality in village flocks dropped from 50 to 8 percent and the population of chickens increased from 900 to 3 500, representing a 250 percent increase (Moerad, 1987). ND vaccines are available in either "live" or "dead" forms:

- **Live vaccines** are fragile and have very precise rules for use, requiring a cold chain up to the point of application to the bird. Their effectiveness is reduced if there are residual antibodies in the chickens. This is especially important with maternal antibodies, which are retained by the newborn chick and protect it for up to ten days. Even a low level of maternal antibody reduces the effectiveness of gaining immunity from the vaccine. Group vaccination can be administered in very clean drinking water in very clean drinkers, or by aerosol (in enclosed buildings). The conventional live vaccine, Hitchner B1, cannot be given in drinking water to village flocks, but can be given using the eye-drop method, which has the advantage that each bird receives its dose individually. This has been successfully carried out in Morocco, where it led to a considerable reduction in mortality (Bell *et al.,* 1990a). The eye-drop method should be used only if there are veterinary personnel available for training vaccinators.

- **Killed vaccines** give good immunity but require priming with a live vaccine for best results, unless a natural infection has already served this purpose. They have been used successfully in Burkina Faso (Verger, 1986, and Ouandaogo, 1990). Killed vaccines have two disadvantages: they must be administered individually by intramuscular injection, which requires some veterinary training, and – as with live vaccines given by eye-drops – the birds must be caught, a cumbersome task which cannot be avoided with the techniques presently available. Killed vaccines have the advantage that they do not require as rigid a cold chain as do live vaccines, and, because they have a consequently longer shelf life, they can be used in more remote locations. They appear to be most effective in birds that have already acquired some degree of immunity from natural NDV exposure or an initial live vaccine inoculation. Another advantage of killed vaccine is that the virus-killing chemical used in its preparation also acts against all other possible vaccine pollutants, such as unwanted viruses, bacteria and other micro-organisms. Killed vaccines are usually cheaper than live vaccines because the product is more durable, but this is only viable for large flocks. Evidence from Burkina Faso and Niger indicates that because each vial contains at least 100 individual doses, there was a high degree of wastage, as the villagers only managed to vaccinate a few dozen birds a day at best. Much of the advantage gained in efficient manufacturing, packaging and dispatching can be lost at this final stage if the contents of the vial are not fully utilized.

### *Constraints to rural flock vaccination*

The low success rate of ND vaccination is almost entirely due to inactivation of the vaccine because of the absence of an efficient cold chain. This in turn is aggravated by the scattered distribution of village flocks, bad road conditions and lack of transport. In Indonesia, the period between the vaccine leaving a central laboratory and vaccination in the village can be several days.

Vaccination programmes should be carried out at appropriate times. There are seasonal patterns to outbreaks of ND and Fowl Pox, the diseases for which vaccination campaigns are usually carried out. The farming programme should be taken into consideration. In Thailand, for example, ND vaccinations are carried out in the dry season when the farmers are not involved with rice cultivation (Danvivatanaporn, 1987).

It has frequently been said that lack of motivation is a major cause of the low vaccination rates in rural areas. To overcome this problem, a pilot project in Thailand organized a training course in primary schools for children of 12 years of age. They were introduced to the concept of the advantages of vaccination against ND and taught to recognise the simple clinical signs of the disease. Another training course for livestock volunteers was given to five selected young village leaders. Upon return to their village, they gave their services and advice on ND control to the village, free of charge. It was hoped that the increased knowledge and commitment would result in better motivation of the villagers to develop their own vaccination programmes.

In Bangladesh, the subdistrict livestock officer organizes special training in vaccination and livestock husbandry, in consultation with the local subdistrict committee chairman and members, who then select the farmers and volunteers for vaccinator training. The course is divided into two phases: theoretical and practical. On completion, the vaccinators are supplied (at cost) with vacuum flasks and other necessary equipment, to vaccinate their own and other villagers' flocks, for a fee. They then return the empty vials and receive fresh vaccine. The Department of Livestock Services runs the livestock disease control programme for small farmers as part of its poultry development programme, usually with the assistance of local non-government organization (NGO) groups (Bangladesh Department of Livestock Services, personal communication 2000).

### *The ND V4 vaccine*

This is a new vaccine, which has the following advantages:

- It is a heat-tolerant vaccine selected from non-virulent forms of NDV naturally occurring in Australasia. In an experiment conducted in Malawi, young chicks which received the vaccine after it had been exposed to ambient temperature for six weeks developed high antibody titres and resisted challenge with a velogenic, viscerotropic ND virus strain (Sagild and Spalatin, 1982).
- After about half of the birds of a household flock are caught and vaccinated, and if all the birds are then confined together overnight, the vaccine will spread naturally from vaccinated to unvaccinated birds. The antibody response of these "naturally" vaccinated is comparable with that of the vaccinated birds (Young, 1991).
- Unlike conventional vaccines, which cannot be given if the birds are under stress, the ND V4 is so mild that it can be given to birds under stress.
- The vaccine can be administered by mixing with feed, although the eye-drop method of inoculation is much more effective.

Alders *et al.* (1994) reported a laboratory vaccine trial with the heat tolerant V4 and the Hitchner B1, in which vaccination with the Heat Resistant (HR) V4 gave slightly higher HI (Haemaglutination Inhibition) titres than vaccination with the Hitchner vaccine. The live HRV4 vaccine was used successfully in the control of ND in village chicken flocks in Malawi (Saglid and Haresnape, 1987). In these field trials, vaccinated birds showed a good immune response when the vaccine was administered through very clean drinking water in very clean drinkers. However, this method can only be used in the dry season, because of the difficulty of confining the birds in completely dry conditions during the rainy season.

A Heat Resistant derivative of the V4 vaccine added to feed was used successfully in Southeast Asia (Copland, 1987). It did not require individual doses, and it spread between birds to some extent. The choice of feed to be used as the vaccine carrier was crucial. Commercial feed as a vaccine carrier has two disadvantages: firstly, its composition varies, and certain components can prove toxic to the vaccine virus; and secondly, prepared feeds are expensive, and one of the essential factors in a smallholder poultry vaccination scheme must be low cost.

In Malaysia, the vaccine is sprayed onto wheat while it is being mixed in a simple, locally manufactured auger-driven mixer. Up to 10 000 doses of vaccine can be mixed at a time. The feed-virus mixture is then put into small plastic bags, each containing 200 g (enough for 20 birds). Even after 45 days storage at ambient temperatures, the bagged vaccine provides up to 90 percent protection.

In other Asian countries where wheat is not readily available, rice has been used. Both rice and wheat have a water-soluble viral inhibitor in the grain coat; thus washed grain maintains a higher virus titre than unwashed grain. Washing is carried out by soaking the grain for 24 hours and then mixing the vaccine with the wet grain. At the village level, the required amount of washed grain (10 g per bird) is measured into a plastic bag and the vaccine added. After mixing thoroughly, the feed-vaccine mixture is fed directly to chickens. It is important to provide creep-feeding for the chicks and growers, otherwise the older birds get all the vaccine.

The V4 strain is being tested in several African countries (Ethiopia, the Gambia, the United Republic of Tanzania, Zimbabwe and Nigeria). The first field test of HRV4 (Heat Resistant V4) was conducted in the Gambia (Jagne *et al.*, 1991). In July 1993, FAO and the governments of the Gambia and Ethiopia signed a Technical Cooperation Programme project agreement, "Assistance to Rural Women in protecting their chicken flocks from Newcastle disease" (TCP/RAF/2376T). The objectives were to introduce and evaluate, under African rural conditions, the HRV4 oral vaccine, which had proved effective in Southeast Asia, and to involve rural women in the implementation of the project. In both countries, repeated oral vaccination (up to four times at regular intervals) did not generally produce the high immunity found in Southeast Asia. However, parallel groups inoculated by eye-drop did achieve high levels of immunity.

In 1995, confined laboratory trials of ND HRV4 feed-based vaccines were carried out in Ethiopia. Oral vaccination, administered in barley, wheat and crushed maize feeds, was compared with eye-drop vaccination and with an unvaccinated control. Eight days after the birds were challenged by the ND virus, the survival rates were: 80 percent of the eye-drop vaccination group; 20 percent of the oral vaccination groups; and none of the control group. Of the three feeds used in the oral vaccination trials, barley proved to be the most efficient vaccine carrier in terms of providing disease resistance, followed by maize and lastly wheat.

Zimbabwe was free of ND from 1986 until 1994, when suddenly infection was introduced from South Africa. Because of unrestricted poultry transport, it spread rapidly across most of the country. During 1994/95, ten million rural chickens nationwide were vaccinated at a project cost of US$1.50 per bird. In early 1996, a FAO-assisted Technical Cooperation Programme was initiated to establish a community-based programme for the prevention of ND epidemics in rural chickens. The approach combined the immediate administration of the V4 vaccine using the conventional eye-drop vaccination method with community-based trials using the feed-mixed oral method under Zimbabwe conditions. Thus it was hoped to avert other epidemics and generate data for planning regular feed-based vaccination of rural chickens as part of the veterinary extension service.

Although V4 has shown promising results in overcoming the major constraints associated with ND vaccination, there are still problems with its use in scavenging systems at the village level, where feeding is irregular and poultry are hatched, bought and sold throughout the year. In all countries, laboratory trials to assess various feeds as carriers and to familiarize technicians with the vaccine and virulent challenge systems should be conducted before field trials. Production data should be collected before, during and after vaccination. This is essential to evaluate the efficiency of vaccination.

## Traditional poultry disease control in Africa

Traditional treatment and control of disease is important, as most developing countries cannot afford to import or subsidize veterinary drugs and vaccines for smallholder farms. There is also increasing concern about the effect of synthetic drugs on animals and the environment. Ojeniyi (1985) found a correlation between the use of antibiotics and drug resistance among *E. coli* strains isolated from intensively managed poultry at the University of Ibadan, Nigeria. All 1248 *E. coli* strains from the University poultry farm, and 2196 strains from a commercial poultry farm in Ibadan, were resistant to tetracycline, streptomycin and sulphonamide. In contrast, all 2284 strains isolated from free-range town and village poultry were sensitive to these drugs.

Most of the information presented below on traditional medicine used for poultry has been collected informally (Bizimana, 1994), and has not been scientifically tested. The main reason for its inclusion here is to encourage formal research.

***Viral diseases***

- **Newcastle Disease**: in Nigeria, either *Lageneria vulgaris* or the bark of *Parkia filicoidea* are given to the flock in drinking water (Nwude and Ibrahim, 1980). In Zimbabwe, the leaves of *Cassia didymobotrya* or the latex of *Euphorbia matabelensis* are given in drinking water (Chavunduka, 1976). In the United Republic of Tanzania, in the regions of Arusha and Kilimanjaro, the stem of *Euphorbia candelabrum* Kotschy var. *candelabrum* or the fruit of *Capsicum annuum* together with the leaves of *Iboza multiflora* are given (Minja, 1989).
- **Fowl pox**: in Zimbabwe, the leaves of *Aloe excelsa* are soaked and the extracted fluid is added to drinking water (Chavunduka, 1976). A poultry disease named "*Yoko yoko*" by the Fulani of Mauritania, Mali and Senegal, is a serious epidemic, affecting hens of all ages. The exact cause of the disease is unknown, but Ba (1982) suggested that it might be a type of Fowl Pox. The signs and symptoms, as described by the Fulani, are dejection, breathing difficulties with the emission of the sound *'yok yok'* and sneezing. Obstruction of the nostrils by yellowish crusts makes the birds breathe through their beaks, which are also encrusted. Lack of appetite and purulent conjunctivitis have also been noted. Eventually, the birds suffocate and die. The mortality rate can be as high as 100 percent in growing chickens, but some adults survive. The birds are systematically

slaughtered and the hen house burnt to prevent spread. The symptoms, as described above, are indicative of the "wet" form of Fowl Pox, where eventually the bird suffocates from a cheesy growth in the trachea. The pox lesions are sometimes less obvious in this type of Fowl Pox disease, but they can be found on close examination.

- **Colds**: in Nigeria, *Hibiscus subdariffia* is pounded, mixed with drinking water and given to birds with ruffled feathers (Nwude and Ibrahim, 1980).

***Protozoan diseases***

Coccidiosis: in Nigeria, *Lageneria vulgaris* is dipped in the flocks' drinking water (Nwude and Ibrahim, 1980).

***Bacterial diseases***

Fowl Cholera: in Nigeria, the fruit of *Adansonia digitata* is broken and soaked in the birds' drinking water. The fruit of *Capsicum annuum* is mixed with soot from the ceilings of thatched buildings (Hausa: *Kunkunniya*) and given in drinking water (Nwude and Ibrahim, 1980).

***Metabolic and infectious diseases***

- **Abdominal disorders**: in Nigeria, the young leaves of *Boswellia dalzelii* are chopped and soaked in water, and the extracted fluid is given as a diarrhoea treatment (Nwude and Ibrahim, 1980). In South Africa (Natal Province), *Leonotis leonurus* Ait.f. is given to treat both yellow and green diarrhoea (Watt and Breyer-Brandwijk, 1962). In Southern Africa, farmers use a cold infusion of the leaves of *Aloe saponaria* Haw. to treat enteritis and indigestion in poultry (Watt and Breyer-Brandwijk, 1962). In West Africa, the chopped leaves of *Pergularia extensa* are fed to turkeys suffering from diarrhoea (Dalziel, 1937). In Zimbabwe, the bulb of *Adenium multiflora* is soaked in water for 12 hours, after which the sick animals are drenched to treat for bloody and watery diarrhoea. For the same purpose, the latex of *Aloe chabandii* or *Euphorbia matabelensis* is given in drinking water (Chavunduka, 1976).
- **Blood in the excreta**: in Zimbabwe, the bark of *Cussonia arborea* is soaked in water, and the sick birds are drenched with the fluid (Chavunduka, 1976).

***Poor growth and low production***

In Nigeria, the fruit of *Cucumis pustulatus* is mixed with bran and placed in drinking water to help growth, prevent disease and increase egg production. The fruit of *Cyperus articulatus* is also placed in drinking water (Nwude and Ibrahim, 1980). In West Africa, the fruit of *Cucumis prophetarum* or *C. pustulatus* is placed in drinking water to help growth, prevent disease, discourage predatory hawks and increase egg production (Dalziel, 1937).

***Ectoparasites***

- Various ectoparasites and parasitic diseases: in Nigeria, the dried leaves and twigs of *Guiera senegalensis* Lam. are burned in poultry houses to reduce ectoparasites (Nwude and Ibrahim, 1980). In Bulawayo, Zimbabwe, *Thamnosma africana* Engl. is placed in chicken pens to repel fleas and ants (Watt and Breyer-Brandwijk, 1962).
- Lice: in Nigeria, the leaves of *Bandeiraea simplicifolia* are placed in hen houses to kill lice (Dalziel, 1937; Nwude and Ibrahim, 1980). Ash from the burnt leaves of *Nicotiana rustica, N. tabacum* or *Carica papaya* is rubbed into feathers to protect against infestation (Nwude and Ibrahim, 1980). In Senegal, the leaves of *Calotropis procera* Ait.f. are used to kill lice on poultry (Dalziel, 1937; Watt and Breyer-Brandwijk, 1962).

***Endoparasites***

Worms: in Nigeria, the fruits of *Cucumis prophetarum* and *Solanum nodiflorum* are used by the Hausa people to treat poultry for worms (Nwude and Ibrahim, 1980).

***Others***

Lameness in ducks: in Nigeria, the Hausa people pulverize the leaves of *Momordica balsamina* and mix them with feed to treat ducks for lameness (Nwude and Ibrahim, 1980).

# Chapter 7
# Breed Improvement

**Strategies to develop poultry breeds suitable for family poultry smallholders in tropical countries must differ from those used in intensive production, and should focus on improving indigenous breeds while also making use of pure exotic and cross-bred chickens where appropriate.**

**Conservation of local breeds possessing genetic variations specific to the particular environment is essential for sustainable development. Although they exist as numerically small populations, local breeds are not only highly adapted to the natural environment, but are also an integral part of the lifestyle of the rural people. People, livestock and environment form a delicately balanced but sustainable ecosystem, and thus the potential impact of any intervention to improve production in the traditional system should be predetermined. The situation is less sensitive in peri-urban, industrial and small-scale intensive poultry production, in which rapid improvements can be achieved through well-designed development programmes. The intensive poultry production sector, however, is generally much smaller than the family poultry sector in virtually all developing countries.**

## STRATEGIES FOR BREED IMPROVEMENT

The following two rules should be incorporated into breeding strategies:

- Germplasm in traditional conditions should not be modified until management and housing have been improved and, even then, selection should be restricted to local breeds.
- When technical conditions are optimum and a ready market exists for the products, then improved breeds, crosses and hybrid strains that have been selected for high performance can be introduced into the peri-urban system, even at small-scale levels.

The most common method of improving the local gene pool is crossing indigenous and exotic birds, and then leaving the hybrid offspring to natural selection. Pure-bred or hybrid cockerels (or pullets) selected for greater meat or egg production are introduced into local flocks, usually in order to increase egg production. It is important to note that improved growth (for meat production) and high egg production are genetically incompatible in the same bird. The genetic traits are negatively correlated, which means that selection for one trait will reduce the other.

### Cockerel or pullet exchange

An example of this type of strategy is a flock of indigenous local hens laying 50 eggs a year and beginning to lay at 25 weeks of age, crossed with "improved breed" cockerels, which have a genetic breed potential of 250 eggs a year, with hens beginning to lay at 21 weeks. The results are cross-bred hybrid pullets beginning to lay at 24 weeks, with a genetic potential of laying 200 eggs per year. The first generation hybrid cross-breed has a higher theoretical genetic potential (genotype) than the average (150) of the two parent breeds, due to the effect of hybrid vigour. However, unless management (especially in the area of nutrition) is improved, this genetic potential will not be realized by the hybrid cross-breed in actual practice in the environment.

If subsequent generations of the hybrid cross-bred pullets are mated (back-crossed) again with the same "improved breed" cockerel, the genetic potential for increased production is raised, although at a slower rate (as hybrid vigour only works with first-time crossing). With each generation, higher levels of management (including the provision of properly balanced feeds) are required to achieve this potential.

If the hybrid cross-breeds mate among themselves, however, potential production falls in the very next generation to the average potential of the two original genotypes, even if management could support the higher hybrid level.

The use of cockerels in this way is the basis for the Cock or Cockerel Exchange Programme (CEP) or Opération Coq, which has been implemented in almost all tropical countries. Households exchange all their local cockerels for a few improved cockerels, which are then raised to maturity to allow them to adapt to local conditions.

In some cases, a Pullet Exchange or Hybrid Hatchable Eggs Programme is used. These approaches were used extensively from the early 1930s until the 1960s, by which time urban development had begun to give rise to peri-urban, intensive, small- to medium-scale poultry production, which makes use of imported commercial breeds and technology.

The gradual replacement of local genes through cross-breeding and artificial selection has been the basis of initial development in many countries (Omeje and Nwosu, 1986; Coligado *et al.*, 1986).

Although many strategies deemed appropriate for smallholder poultry production systems have been implemented, most have not succeeded, due to a lack of management input to support the improved potential.

## Replacement of all indigenous breeds

The use of hybrid chickens under free-range rural conditions has often been studied, notably in Zimbabwe (Huchzermeyer, 1973), and in Sri Lanka, Zambia and Nicaragua (Roberts and Senaratne, 1992; de Vries, 1995).

It has consistently been found that entire flock replacement programmes lead to increased egg and meat production, but only where management supplies good nutrition and veterinary hygiene. There is, however, one great disadvantage, in that the use of commercial hybrids to increase egg production necessarily eliminates broodiness of hens, due to the negative genetic correlation between these two factors. For this reason, complete replacement of local birds should not be considered unless a reliable local supply of day-old chicks (of an appropriate breed) is available.

## Selection within local breeds

### *Production traits of local breeds*

The genetic development of local breeds and varieties in developing countries first requires proper documentation of their productive and reproductive performance. The main production characteristics of local breeds are:

- small body size (low nutritional maintenance requirement);
- lateness in maturing (up to 36 weeks of age);
- low performance in egg numbers (20 to 50) and egg size (25 to 45 g);
- small clutch sizes (two to ten eggs); and
- long pauses between laying of clutches and a predominant inclination to broodiness.

For rural smallholder extensive systems, meat production cannot be separated from egg or chick production, and thus a highly broody (with consequent low egg production), low body-weight (low-feed requirement) bird is best for survival under these conditions. Surplus cockerels, whatever they weigh, are usually sold for meat when they reach sexual maturity at three to four months of age. Under rural smallholder extensive systems, there is little reproductive control of the hens, as they brood their own chicks for continuous regeneration of the flock. The egg brooding (incubation) and chick rearing activity increases the reproductive cycle length by 58 days to about 74 days in total:

16 days for egg laying and clutch formation + 21 days for hatching + 37 days (5.3 weeks) for chick rearing = 74 days

Source: Horst, 1990b

Thus, most hens can produce chicks about four to five times per year, and only four times if the rearing period is extended to eight weeks. As malnutrition, infections, predators and accidents result in mortality rates of 60 to 70 percent during rearing, virtually all eggs are used for reproduction. With four to five reproductive cycles per year, only about nine replacement pullets may be obtained.

Fertility and hatchability are also high in local birds. They generally adapt well to unfavourable management conditions, and resistance to prevailing diseases is usually assumed to be high, although juvenile and sometimes adult mortality rates can be high in extensive production systems.

Considerable genetic differences exist between different regional and continental populations of indigenous chickens, and production rates of local populations should be evaluated before introducing development programmes.

### *Selection programmes for local breeds*

Although better management procedures can significantly improve the performance of local birds, some feel there is also a need for genetic selection (Nwosu, 1979). Pure-breeding and selection programmes have been developed in Bangladesh (Ahmad and Hashnath, 1983), although not implemented in the field. Both of the above groups concluded that although improvement of local poultry breeds would be beneficial, it is essential to evaluate breeds and their crosses before undertaking a breeding strategy.

Research conducted in the United Republic of Tanzania (Katule, 1991) concluded that selection for dual-purpose characteristics within individual local populations is both time-consuming and costly. Cross-breeding with improved breeds is recommended, followed by selection in the composite population.

Although consumer preference in most developing countries is for dual-purpose breeds, it is important to restate that in the same bird, the traits of increased egg production and increased broodiness are genetically incompatible, as are the traits of high egg production and high meat production. Selection for any trait within these pairs will reduce the other trait of that pair.

## Modifying local breeds using major gene types

The use of single or combined dominant genes for feather restriction (Na) and feathering structure (F), as well as the sex-linked recessive gene for reduced body size (dw), has been found to be particularly relevant for the tropics (Horst, 1989; Haaren-Kiso *et al.*, 1995). Research into the effects of these genes on economic factors has been undertaken in Malaysia (Khadijah, 1988; Mathur and Horst, 1989). For example, the feather restriction (Na) or Naked Neck gene results in 40 percent less feather coverage overall, with the lower neck appearing almost "naked". This considerably reduces the need for dietary nutrition to supply protein input for feather production, and protein is a limiting factor in many scavenger feed resource bases. Barua *et al.*, (1998) has reviewed the available information on the performance of indigenous Naked Neck fowl in the hope that it will draw the attention of scientists worldwide to its interesting characteristics and facilitate future research.

The incorporation of such genes could be significant in the development of appropriate breeds and strains for smallholder poultry production in the tropics. There are now seven potentially useful major genes:

- Na - naked neck (autosomal -A);
- Dw - dwarf (sex-linked -S);
- K - slow feathering (S);
- Fa - Fayoumi (A);

- F - frizzle (A);
- H - silky (A); and
- Fm - fibro-melanosis (A).

The use of major genes to improve productivity in smallholder poultry breeding programmes has been researched in various tropical countries (including Indonesia, Malaysia, Thailand, Bangladesh, Bolivia, India, Cameroon and Nigeria).

Other morphological traits that allow better heat dissipation include large combs, large wattles and long legs. Gene coding for these traits, which are not major genes but the result of multiple genes and their interactions, could also be considered for incorporation into the development of high performance local birds for the tropics.

## BETTER PRODUCTION: BY BREEDING OR MANAGEMENT?

Family poultry is well integrated into most village farming systems, with local breeds representing 40 to 70 percent of the national meat and egg supply in most tropical countries. Because of their scavenger adaptability, production ability and low cost, local breeds are kept by rural smallholders, landless farmers and industrial labourers. It is difficult to imagine birds better adapted for survival under scavenger free-range conditions than the breeds that have already evolved under those very same conditions, and are still surviving as proof of their ability to do so. However, there does remain a considerable and largely unexploited potential for increased production from local breeds through improved management.

The critical management objective for scavenger free-range systems is to reduce the high mortality in both growing and adult age groups, but especially the 60 to 70 percent mortality in the growers. This high mortality means that many eggs laid by the hen need to be used for reproduction to maintain flock size, instead of for sale or consumption. It also means that many birds that die could instead be sold or consumed as meat.

The problem with local breeds, as outlined above, is not inherently low egg production or low meat production, but high mortality. Breed improvement to increase meat or egg production would not solve the health and nutrition management problems. However, increased egg production (by breed improvement) would create a new problem – lack of broodiness in the flock – which would force the smallholder to buy stock rather than have the hen brood and rear her own.

Mortality can be significantly reduced through increasing farmer awareness of health needs, through the provision of vaccine (especially for Newcastle Disease) and through improving the nutrition of growing stock (for example, by providing creep feeding systems). These are the most important improvements to management activities that will enable to the farmer to best exploit the existing potential of local breeds under scavenging free-range conditions.

If management resources available to the smallholder or landless farmer increase to the extent of a local supply of balanced poultry feed, the options open to his income-generating ability are increased. However, the answer is not to confine local breeds in intensive management systems. The performance of local breeds will increase slightly under cage or deep litter management (Akinokun, 1975; Oluyemi, 1979; Nwosu, 1979) but, because the genetic potential for egg production (or meat production) of local breeds is lower than that of commercial hybrids, the same investment in intensive management will achieve a much higher production result by using commercial hybrids.

If balanced feed, good health-care supplies and day-old chicks of hybrid varieties are locally available, then intensive poultry management is an option. If these are not available, raising local breeds under scavenger free-range systems is still the best choice.

The vast potential for increasing income generation from scavenger free-range family poultry clearly lies in the management area of reducing mortality in growing chickens. This alone is sufficient challenge for the already overstretched resources of government and NGO field extension staff in developing countries.

The potential for breed improvement is a factor to be considered in the future, but only when the more immediate objective of reducing mortality is attained. Meanwhile efforts should be continued to preserve germplasm as a resource for the future.

# Chapter 8
# Production Economics

The agricultural subsector of animal production is part of a complex interdependent farming system. Analysis of livestock production cannot be based solely on input and output, but must also take into consideration other farming activities. The interaction between animal production and other subsectors can be complementary, as in the use of manure; or competitive, as in the allocation of land to crops or livestock grazing.

The farming system as a whole, and animal production in particular, is influenced by external factors (including government policy on rural development, livestock development programmes and marketing), which must be considered in any analysis or evaluation.

## DEFINITION AND ANALYSIS OF PRODUCTION COSTS

The farming system is defined as the combination of all farm enterprises/subsystems, management and farmer objectives and the interaction between them. It is a decision-making and land-use unit, comprising the farming household and the crop and livestock systems, which transforms land, labour, management and capital into products that can be consumed or sold.

Enterprises/subsystems are defined as the different subdivisions of the farming system, each producing one kind of crop or livestock product. In the case of family poultry, the products are poultry meat and eggs, with manure as a by-product. The harvesting of family poultry for home consumption and sale can be considered as the management of a standing resource for economic yield. In this respect, the economic principles applying to the management of fauna, parklands, fisheries, wood and timber forests and rangelands are more appropriate than the economic concepts more commonly applied to the labour and capital-dependent livestock production and other commercial farming industries.

## METHODS AND CRITERIA FOR COST CALCULATION

The cost of production can be seen from various angles. The inputs may be external (Non-Factor costs) or internal (Factor costs). Internal input is under the control of the farming household, and includes land, labour, management and capital. The cash involved in production represents either Cash (Paid) Costs or Non-Cash (Calculated) Costs. Another way to categorize the costs is to distinguish Variable Costs from Fixed Costs. Variable costs rise and fall with the size of the output and the level of the operation. Variable costs (for items such as feed, vaccine and casual labour) can be controlled to some extent and are not incurred when there is no production. Fixed costs (for items such as taxes, insurance, interest, and depreciation on buildings and equipment), are incurred whether or not there is any output.

The Opportunity Cost principle is applied in farm cost accounting. Opportunity costs can be defined as the "income that would have been generated if the production resource/input/factor were put to the next best alternative use". Many farm enterprises/subsystems yield more than one product. Poultry produce eggs, meat and manure. When calculating the cost-price per unit of production, the cash value of the by-products (sold externally or used as a substitute in another enterprise/subsystem of the farm), must be subtracted from the Total Gross Costs. This will result in the Total Net Costs. For the cost-price per unit of production, the Total Net Costs must be divided by the total number of units of production.

The cost-price calculation model splits production costs into two categories: Paid Costs and Calculated Costs. Paid costs involve actual payment in cash or kind for inputs or services used. Calculated costs are determined using mathematical formulae, and include the following:

- depreciation on the poultry house and equipment;
- interest on cash in hand and personal capital used to construct the poultry house and purchase equipment, birds and feed;

- maintenance of the poultry house and equipment; and
- labour supplied by the farm family.

Calculated Costs include Opportunity Costs as related to the national economy: for example, unemployment (including hidden unemployment) and high rates of devaluation of the national currency. These form a part of the socio-economic reality for the smallholder, and influence the Opportunity Cost of labour (reduced by high unemployment) and of capital (which tends to move towards zero when the rate of currency devaluation is higher than the interest rate). By making use of locally available and renewable materials for poultry housing and equipment, family poultry producers minimize the introduction of external capital into their enterprise.

Large-scale poultry production cannot really be compared with smallholder family poultry, because smallholders often face such constraints as the absence of organized marketing systems and the lack of price rewards for produce quality and uniformity. Therefore, the cost-price calculation for large-scale poultry production (and also that for free-range commercial poultry production) may not be applicable to smallholder family poultry systems without modifications.

Elson (1992) showed that for layers, production costs (per dozen eggs produced) increased with space allowance (stock density) per hen. The minimum stock density allowed in the EC (under EEC Council directive 1988/66) is 22 birds/m$^2$ (450 cm$^2$/bird). The production cost for birds housed in laying cages at this density is used as a baseline. The percent increases in cost over this baseline (each with their associated management system) are:

- 5 percent for aviaries;
- 7–12 percent for percheries (tiered wire floor aviaries) at 20 birds/m$^2$;
- 15 percent for cages at 20 birds/m$^2$ (750 cm$^2$/bird);
- 21 percent for deep litter systems at 7 birds/m$^2$;
- 30 percent for straw yards at 3 birds/m$^2$;
- 35 percent for semi-intensive systems at 0.1 birds/m$^2$ (1000 birds/ha);
- 50 percent for free-range systems at 0.04 birds/m$^2$ (400 birds/ha).

A comparison of the EC cage minimum as a base, with perchery and free-range alternatives, is shown in Table 8.1.

(Calculations were made using feed at £140/tonne; pullets at £2.35 each; old hens at 24.2p/kg)

## A BROADER ECONOMIC FRAMEWORK FOR ANALYSIS

All economic activity consists of transforming resources (land, labour and capital) into goods and services which serve the needs and desires of people. Much of the quantitative assessment in cost-benefit analysis is simple accountancy: assigning monetary values to various measured or estimated physical quantities, categorizing them under a cost or benefit heading, adding them up, and finally comparing the totals. Proper economic analysis should provide a framework by which the benefits of production are shown in the economic system, and how these benefits are valued by society. This can only be done with a "before and after" or "with or without" analysis.

Benefits can be measured in two ways:

- by a **technical** component which represents the higher productivity of resources used (and hence reduced unit costs) in supplying poultry products; and
- an **economic** component which reflects the value placed by society on those supplies.

**Table 8.1** Performance and production costs of three alternative systems in the United Kingdom

| | System | | |
|---|---|---|---|
| | **Cage** | **Perch** | **Free-range** |
| **Performance** | | | |
| Stock density | 22 | 20 | 0.04 |
| Eggs per hen housed | 276 | 265 | 252 |
| Feed intake, g/bird/day | 115 | 116 | 135 |
| Mortality, % | 5 | 5 | 8 |
| Old hen weight, kg | 2.2 | 2.2 | 2.3 |
| No of birds/worker | 20 000 | 10 000 | 2 500 |
| **Production costs** (pence per dozen eggs) | | | |
| Feed | 25.5 | 27.8 | 32.8 |
| Bird depreciation | 7.9 | 8.4 | 8.6 |
| Labour | 1.5 | 3.2 | 13.3 |
| Electricity | 1.2 | 1.2 | 0.7 |
| Medication | 0.1 | 0.1 | 0.2 |
| Other costs | 1.1 | 1.2 | 1.3 |
| **Total** | 37.4 | 41.8 | 56.9 |

Source: Elson (1992), as quoted by Tucker (1989)

The technical effects are demonstrated in an economic analysis as a shift of the supply curve - the basic relationship showing the minimum price at which different levels of production can be made available to the market. This is shown in Figure 8.1 as the downward shift in the curve $S_0$ to $S_1$. The value placed on this change in potential availability is then entirely dependent on the demand for poultry products. With rising demand for these products, additional supplies become expensive, and therefore the extra production translates into a substantial gain in benefits to the community. It can be argued that this usually happens in developing countries where, compared to the staple diet, poultry products are a luxury commodity with a relatively higher value. Hence, the demand curve D shows that the quantity demanded is highly responsive to price and income changes, with additional consumption causing little decrease in value. The demand for poultry products is price/income elastic.

This simple model highlights the overall economic impact of higher poultry production as manifested on the market for poultry products. Production and consumption rise from $Q_0$ to $Q_1$ but the average price paid by consumers (and received by producers) falls from $P_0$ to $P_1$. Consumers gain significantly, reaping the benefits of both greater supplies and lower prices. Producers also gain. Although unit costs fall, the increase in production compensates for the price reduction and, as evident from the diagram, total revenue received by producers, ($P_1Q_1$) is greater than the previous $P_0Q_0$.

The overall net economic benefit from improved family poultry production technology is represented by the size of the shaded area. It is this net economic benefit that an economic analysis of family poultry development schemes and programmes should be seeking to estimate.

**Fig. 8.2** A representation of the market for poultry products from smallholders

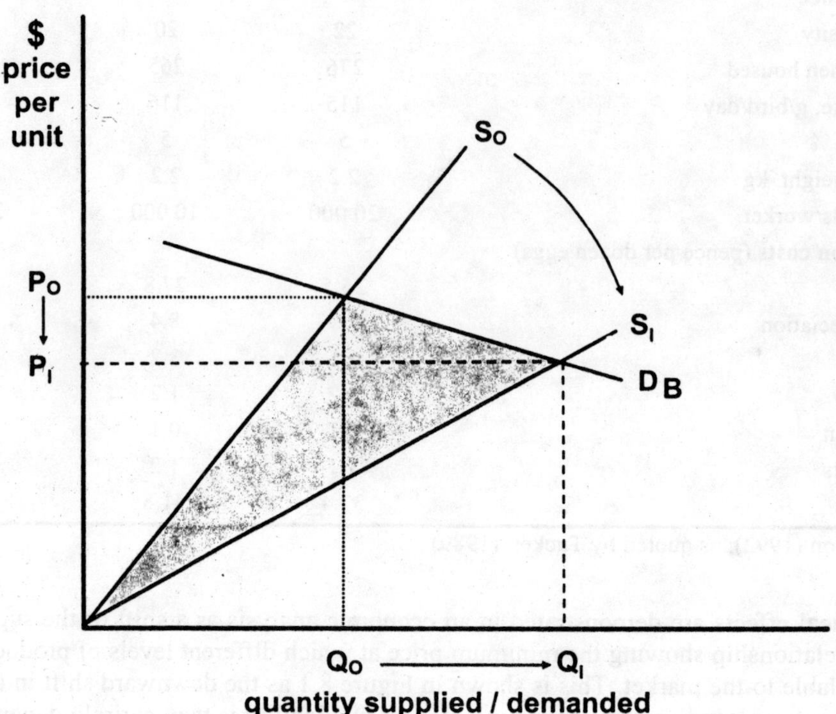


Image for demand-supply curve

# Chapter 9
# Marketing

As a country develops, more of its consuming population lose touch with the village and food producers. Thus more specialised marketing services are needed. Farm produce must be collected, packed and transported in good condition to the cities and distributed to retailers near consumers' homes. This also calls for grading and storage of the product. The more developed the country becomes; the greater is the variety of products that can be economically produced. All this must be provided at a cost that consumers can afford.

A study of existing marketing systems in a country will often reveal how they have evolved to their present state. Many developing countries do not have refrigeration as a factor in their storage, either during transport, retail or consumer household stages. For this reason, poultry meat is purchased live, and slaughtered immediately before consumption. Also, eggs are often retailed with a means for the buyer to check their quality before buying, either by "candling" (to see the internal quality with a lantern or battery-torch) or a bucket of water (to test the egg's age by the floatation method). Both methods essentially test for the size of the air-cell situated at the blunt end of the egg, which increases in size as moisture is lost from the egg. With a bigger air-cell, there is more floatation.

In developing countries, transport of eggs and poultry from the village to the city usually begins with a purchase by a middleman dealer, direct from the household, or from small locally held weekly markets. Baskets with layers of straw protect the eggs from breakage, and other types of baskets are used to carry live birds. Bullock carts are still used in many countries for transport of both live poultry and eggs to larger community centres. The roofs of buses or trains replace these slower vehicles as transport systems develop. Marketing quality considerations for live birds are usually concerned with weight loss in the bird from dehydration during transport. These are easily resolved by providing drinking water during the trip, and travelling during the cool part of the day when possible. Egg quality considerations are more complex and are dealt with in the second half of this chapter.

Improved marketing programmes must add no more cost to the product than the consumer can afford. Important marketing improvements can often be simply made by making small corrections to already existing handling, transport, packaging, grading and storage methods.

Marketing organisations generally come into being very gradually, and must be appropriate for the background, character and education of the people concerned. Plans for radical changes, which do not take sufficient account of social and economic environments, are likely to fail. Thus any improvement programme should be designed to achieve desirable modifications in existing commercial facilities (and their economic and legal framework) by a process of steady growth.

As a country develops, the task of marketing eggs and poultry will still involve the collection of live poultry and eggs from farmers, transporting them to a grading, packing or processing plant, grading and standardising the poultry meat and eggs, processing them and packaging them into more useful forms, storing them (preferably under refrigeration), moving them through wholesale and retail channels and delivering them to consumers at a convenient time and place.

This chapter provides a brief outline with some practical information and advice to those who are immediately concerned with egg and poultry marketing considerations. For a more detailed examination of marketing, the reader is referred to FAO Marketing Guide N° 4 "Marketing eggs and poultry" (1961), from which some of the following material is taken.

## FACTORS AFFECTING DEMAND FOR POULTRY MEAT AND EGGS

### Ceremonial and traditional aspects

In traditional societies, poultry are often used for ceremonies, sacrifices and gifts. What follows are some traditional aspects of poultry keeping from the Mossi of Burkina Faso (West Africa), the Mamprusi of northern Ghana, and Bangladeshi and Malay farmers in South Asia.

Among the Mossi people when no poultry is available (such as after a Newcastle Disease outbreak), to meet customary family obligations, the household must purchase or borrow a bird. Chickens are given to convey value to a relationship, or to offer thanks for a favour or help (such as from government officials). For most socio-cultural and religious purposes, the required sex and colour of fowls are also prescribed. For example, a family will give a white cockerel when an agreement for marriage is reached.

The consumption of eggs in Mossi villages is uncommon. There is a strong belief that a child who regularly eats eggs will become a thief, reasoning that the good taste of eggs will make the child want to eat eggs often. The only eggs consumed are those that fail to hatch under broody hens. These are boiled and then eaten. Chicken eggs, unlike guinea fowl eggs, are not part of the trade in poultry products, since all eggs are required for hatching to maintain the flock (given the normally high losses during rearing). Dealers from urban areas reflect the demand for village eggs. The eggs are often bought by small food stall merchants who boil the eggs and resell them as snack food. A considerable number of guinea fowl eggs are collected by the Mossi for sale, most of which find their way to the cities via village markets, where dealers buy the eggs.

The Mamprusi society in northern Ghana has a variety of uses for poultry products. Chicken cocks are the most popular sacrificial animals. Guinea fowl cocks are not used. The colour of the bird is important. A red cock is sacrificed to ask for rain or a good harvest; a white cock is used to convey value in relationships, and a black cock is used to ask for protection against disease, war or quarrels. Because of these customs, red, white and black cocks have double the value of cocks of other colours.

The sale of young birds and eggs takes place in the Mamprusi village markets. Prices fluctuate during the year, and are low during the pre-harvest season, when the granaries are empty and the crops are still growing and thus cash is less available. At such times, traders from the south come to buy for resale in the cities. Sometimes, middlemen dealers are involved. They buy the birds in the villages and sell them at markets or to city-based traders. The sale of poultry products from Mamprusi households contributes about 15 percent to Mamprusi annual cash income.

Poultry consumption by the household is rare, as most birds are sold for income generation. In Mamprusi society, women, circumcised girls and first-born children do not consume eggs or meat. These products are only eaten by elderly men, male visitors and young children. The reasons are not fully understood. Some Mamprusi women believe that during pregnancy, their behaviour (including their food choices) can affect their unborn child.

In Bangladesh, eggs and meat are consumed mainly by men and boys, and very rarely by women and girls. Low-income groups generally do not consume eggs or meat. These products are sold, and from the proceeds, essential items are purchased, such as carbohydrate and low-cost vegetable protein foods.

Guinea fowl, more than chicken, are given as gifts to visitors. To give a gift is considered to be a wealth-increasing action as well as an act that conveys value on the receiver. Farmers often save for agricultural equipment or other materials and small livestock is used as a savings account. The offspring, like chicks, are considered to be the interest on the savings.

In many parts of Africa, birds are sold to meet unforeseen expenses, for example, to buy the beer and kola-nuts customarily given to gravediggers when a family member dies. The birds usually sold from the village flock are: surplus males (cockerels and cocks); pullets; old hens; non-productive hens; large-sized birds and sick birds. Young birds are often sold just before the onset of the high-risk period for Newcastle Disease.

## Traditional taste values placed on poultry meat

It is important to understand traditional taste values and their effect on market demand. The market price for free-range birds for meat is usually stable because:

- the meat is considered tastier and stronger flavoured than commercial broiler meat;
- the meat (muscle tissue) is tougher, and retains its texture when prepared in dishes requiring longer cooking; and
- the birds are not fed with compounded feed which may contain antibiotics, anti-mould compounds, enzymes, sulpha drugs and other medicines or synthetic chemicals.

In eastern Asia, it is believed that chickens fed with chemicals and drugs have poorer therapeutic value, as they do not combine well with ginseng and other oriental herbs used in making soups, especially steamed types. For this type of soup, younger pullets are preferred and thus they fetch a higher price than do the cockerels. The female is said to be more beneficial and the meat tastier. Steamed chicken soup is believed to provide virility and vigour. It is commonly recommended in Malaysia for pregnant women and for those recovering from sickness.

In the case of large-scale commercial *ayam kampung* (local village chicken) production in Malaysia, local birds are confined and fed on commercial rations but they fetch lower prices than free-range local birds. Such large-scale production has an affect on the market value of all local birds, as purchasers have difficulty distinguishing between genuine free-range and commercially fed local birds. However, the price of *ayam kampung* continues to hold a margin above that of commercial meat chickens. The introduction of more appropriate methods of Newcastle Disease vaccination in Malaysia will reduce mortality at the village level which may also stimulate further interest in family poultry production. If this happens, there will be an increase in the supply of local free-range poultry products to the market, and the price of the *ayam kampung* product (from large-scale commercial production) may fall further.

## Carcass parts and organ meats

The value of birds for sale in developing countries depends firstly on the available supply, secondly on the age and sex of the birds, and thirdly on their size or weight. Young birds, especially cockerels up to six months of age (weighing up to one kilogram live weight), are usually preferred by consumers. This is because larger birds are more expensive for most households, and smaller birds are more tender and have the same preferred portions (drumsticks for example). Table 9.1 shows carcass characteristics of the local village chicken in Bangladesh.

**Table 9.1** Product characteristics of indigenous scavenging chickens in Bangladesh

| Characteristic | Mean |
|---|---|
| Live weight, kg | 1.14 |
| Carcass weight, % | 55 |
| Eggs/hen/year | 35 45 |
| Egg weight, g | 35 – 39 |
| Hatchability of eggs, % | 84 – 87 |

Source: Ahmed, 1994 (Bangladesh Livestock Research Institute)

Whatever the size of bird, all chickens have an equal number of high-demand portions (such as breasts and drumsticks), and a similar proportion of gizzards and other desirable organ parts (see Table 9.2).

**Table 9.2** Organ weights and carcass composition of Ethiopian local chickens at different ages

| Body part weight (grams) | Slaughter age (months) 3 | 4 | 5 | 6 |
|---|---|---|---|---|
| Total body | 502 | 674 | 892 | 1006 |
| Gizzard | 19.9 | 24.1 | 27.7 | 30.9 |
| Heart | 2.6 | 3.1 | 3.8 | 4.1 |
| Intestine | 60.9 | 67.0 | 77.4 | 81.8 |
| Kidneys | 4.6 | 5.4 | 5.6 | 6.4 |
| Liver | 15.8 | 20.0 | 22.9 | 25.9 |
| Lung | 4.0 | 5.1 | 6.2 | 6.6 |
| Pancreas | 1.8 | 2.0 | 2.3 | 2.9 |
| Total organs | 109.6 | 126.7 | 145.9 | 158.6 |
| Body weight % | 21.8 | 18.8 | 16.3 | 15.3 |
| **Carcass** | | | | |
| Bone | 87 | 113 | 123 | 138 |
| Meat | 197 | 267 | 331 | 406 |
| Skin | 36 | 49 | 59 | 68 |
| Total Carcass | 320 | 429 | 513 | 612 |
| Body weight % | 63.7 | 63.6 | 57.5 | 60.8 |

Source: Forssido, 1986

Buying small birds supplies the same number of the desirable parts for a lower price. Together with the tenderness of the meat, this explains the heavier trade in young birds, which are also bought for replacement stock in depleted flocks.

## SUPPLY MECHANISMS FOR POULTRY MEAT AND EGGS

Depending on the location of the farm dwelling, birds and eggs are sold from the household to traders (dealers or middlemen), direct to consumers, or carried by the farmer to the local market. The role of traders in the marketing of poultry products is an important one. Traders from urban areas buy eggs in villages to sell in cities. Where transport is an important consideration (as in many parts of Africa), guinea fowl eggs, with their stronger shells, are preferred to chicken eggs. Prices of eggs are related to supply and demand, to the higher risk of spoilage and lower use for hatching in hot and humid seasons, and to the availability of alternative protein foods such as fish. There is a tendency to hatch less in the hot season, due to low hatchability and diseases of young chickens, and there is also less hatching in the cold season, due to the risk of chilling stress to the young chicks.

Birds are either brought to the local market once or twice a week for sale to local consumers, to other local markets, or to local traders. Chickens are transported to the market in open-weave (well ventilated) baskets or wooden crates. They need not be fed on the day of sale, but should receive drinking water. If the trip to the market takes eight hours or more, stops should be made to supply water to the birds. In hot seasons, it is better to transport birds at night or in the cooler early morning. While the price of live birds depends on their size, the price of eggs depends more on number.

It is often assumed that for poultry and eggs, producers get 60 to 65 percent of the market price but this has been found to be false in Bangladesh, where they receive less than this. The role of traders or hawkers is very important, as it makes selling from the house possible, but these traders take up to 35 percent of the market value, with a consequent lower profit for the farmers who are responsible for production. This loss of income has stimulated farmers in many places to organize sales through their own marketing groups or formal cooperatives.

## Supply channels

A study by Adeyanju *et al.* (undated, unpublished monograph) of the marketing of poultry products in Ondo State (in south-western Nigeria) revealed a large number of transactions and participants. The typical flow of the products from the producer to the consumer is shown in Figure 9.1. The local channel begins with the producer selling poultry products to retailers who serve the needs of local consumers. In most areas, local consumers also buy directly from producers. The other marketing channel involves wholesalers. They buy poultry products directly from producers and sell to retailers inside and outside the State, and are based in urban centres where urban-based consumers are located.

**Fig. 9.1** Supply channel for poultry products in Ondo State, Nigeria

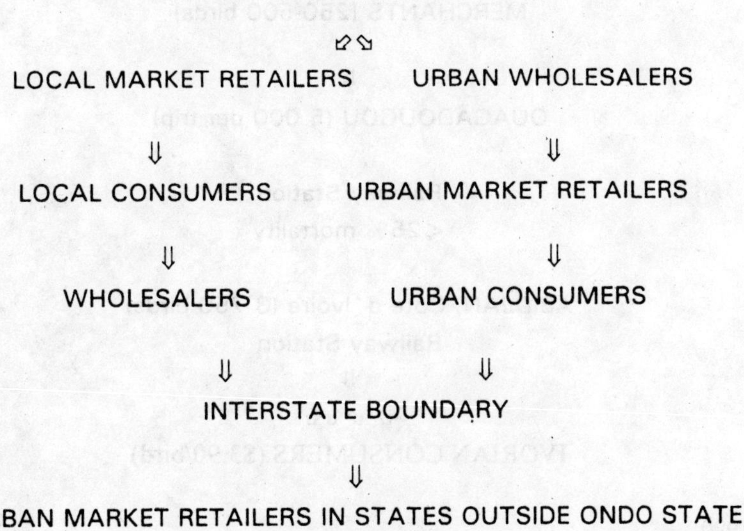


Source: Adeyanju *et al.*, (Poultry Farming in Ondo State, undated, unpublished monograph)

Odi (1990) found that marketing channels for family poultry often cross international boundaries and can generate significant foreign exchange for the producing countries (see Figure 9.2).

**Figure 9.2** Supply channels into Côte d'Ivoire for guinea fowls produced in Burkina Faso

BURKINA PRODUCER HOUSEHOLDS ($1.33/bird)

⇓

PRIMARY COLLECTOR (5-10 birds)

⇓

SECONDARY COLLECTORS (50-100 birds)

⇓

MERCHANTS (250-500 birds)

⇓

OUAGADOUGOU (5 000 per trip)

Railway Station
< 25% mortality

ABIDJAN, Cote d´Ivoire (3 750 birds)
Railway Station

⇓

⇙⇙⇘⇘

IVORIAN CONSUMERS ($3.90/bird)

Source: Odi, 1990

## Planning

Forming a marketing plan means identifying where and when birds and eggs will be sold to receive the best possible prices. Putting large numbers of birds up for sale in a small community may depress the price.

Even the sale of small numbers of intensively managed layers needs advance planning. A flock of 20 hens may produce 1 200 eggs in a year, even at the low production rate of 35 percent. The plans of other farmers must also be considered. If they all expand their flocks and have good years, prices will almost inevitably fall. Seasonal considerations enter into market plans as well. In India for instance, eggs are thought of as a heat-producing food and are eaten in the cool, rainy season. Many factors affect the quality of eggs (see Tables 9.3 to 9.6) and hence the price that consumers are willing to pay for them in the market.

**Table 9.3** Egg quality parameters for four breeds of chickens

| Trait | Nigerian Local | Isa Brown | Trait | Ethiopian Local | White Leghorn |
|---|---|---|---|---|---|
| | (Asuquo *et al.*, 1992) | | | (Forssido, 1986) | |
| Egg wt., g | 40.6 | 59.2 | Egg wt., g | 46.0 | 64.0 |
| Yolk, % | 36.9 | 26.3 | Yolk, % | 36.8 | 34.0 |
| Albumen, % | 52.6 | 62.8 | Albumen, % | 49.6 | 53.0 |
| Shell thickness, mm | 0.30 | 0.35 | Shell thickness, mm | 0.35 | NA |
| Yolk index | 0.36 | 0.46 | Fertility, % | 56.4 | 46.0 |
| Albumen index | 0.09 | 0.12 | Hatchability % | 42.1 | 24.1 |
| Haugh unit | 79.8 | 89.9 | Haugh unit | NA | NA |

**Table 9.4** Length of lay and egg quality in Nigerian indigenous chicken

| Traits | Months of Lay | | | | | |
|---|---|---|---|---|---|---|
| | 2 | 3 | 4 | 5 | 6 | 7 |
| Egg wt, g | 35.8 | 37.2 | 36.9 | 37.1 | 39.0 | 38.6 |
| Yolk wt, g | 14.9 | 14.7 | 14.5 | 14.2 | 14.0 | 14.2 |
| % Albumen | 47.9 | 50.8 | 51.5 | 52.0 | 52.0 | 53.5 |
| Shell thickness, mm | 0.39 | 0.39 | 0.36 | 0.32 | 0.36 | 0.35 |

Source: Olori and Sonaiya, 1992b

**Table 9.5** Quality of eggs of different shell colour of the Nigerian indigenous chicken

| Trait | Brown | Light Brown | White |
|---|---|---|---|
| Egg wt., g | 38.9 | 37.1 | 37.0 |
| Yolk wt., g | 14.5 | 14.0 | 14.8 |
| Shell wt., g | 3.78 | 3.58 | 3.51 |
| Albumen wt., g | 20.6 | 19.6 | 18.8 |
| Shell, % | 9.77 | 9.67 | 9.49 |
| Yolk, % | 37.4 | 37.8 | 39.9 |
| Albumen, % | 52.3 | 52.8 | 50.8 |
| Shell thickness, mm | 0.37 | 0.37 | 0.35 |
| Surface area, $cm^2$ | 52.6 | 50.9 | 50.8 |

Source: Olori and Sonaiya, 1992a

## EGG QUALITY CONSIDERATIONS

Quality determines the acceptability of a product to potential purchasers. The quality of eggs and the preservation of this quality during storage is a function of their physical structure and chemical composition. A basic outline of the most important factors of concern in egg quality is presented below.

### Egg composition

The egg consists of shell, two shell membranes, the white (or albumin) and the yolk. The shell is quite porous to air and water vapour but is very resistant to invasion by micro-organisms as long as it is clean and dry. A thin outer covering on the shell called the "bloom" or "cuticle" (which is unfortunately easily removed by washing), assists this process. After the egg is laid, its contents shrink, both from cooling and water evaporation. Air is drawn in (along with anything else on the shell, such as bacteria or fungi) through the pores in the shell to replace this loss. A gap opens up between the two membranes because the outer one is attached to the shell and the inner one is attached to the egg white. This gap is known as the "air cell" and is usually found at the large blunt end of the egg. The egg white takes the form of a "thick" albumin sack enclosing the yolk, with a more fluid "thin" albumin between this sack and the yolk to the inside, and again between the sack and the shell to the outside. These layers provide a barrier to prevent the yolk touching the shell and to provide food for the embryo. Egg white has specific antibiotic effects, which further protect the yolk. Egg white also contains two fibrous cords (the chalaza), which are attached to the yolk and to either end of the egg, which help hold the yolk in the centre and assist in preventing the yolk from touching the shell.

The weight of an egg laid by a local village breed of hen is about 35 g. Commercial hybrids lay eggs of about 58 g weight. The shell comprises approximately 11 percent of the weight of an egg, the remainder being the edible portion. By weight of edible portion, the yolk is 36 percent and the white is 64 percent.

## Shell quality

Eggs of unusual shape are more likely to be damaged during the marketing process, and consumers do not like them. Small thin cracks in the shell, which do not leak, are called "checks". These are usually detected by candling. "Checked" eggs should be sold for immediate consumption, as their storage life is limited. The household usually consumes eggs with leaking cracks, where the eggshell membranes are broken as well as the shell. Brittle, thin-shelled eggs (shells less than 0.35 mm thick) are also unsuitable for transport to market. Dirty eggs must be cleaned by dry or wet methods, and thus have a higher marketing risk because of the removal of the cuticle.

Shell colour is not a guide to egg quality, but there is usually a consumer bias to either white or brown, which must be considered in marketing.

## Egg yolk and egg white quality

Consumers prefer the odour and flavour of normal fresh eggs. The yolk should be round, firm and yellow in colour. Local yolk colour preferences may vary and can be easily adjusted by raising or lowering the amount of green leaf material included in the poultry ration or supplement. Egg white normally has a slightly yellow-green tinge and the thick white is slightly cloudy.

Consumers are usually critical of blood or meat spots, which can vary in colour from red to grey, and in size from small specks up to one square centimetre. Blood spots are caused by slight bleeding at the time of release of the ovule (yolk) from the ovary of the hen. They may be found in the white or adhering to the yolk.

## Deterioration

The interior quality of eggs deteriorates after laying at a rate depending on time and conditions of storage, such as temperature, relative humidity (RH), and the presence of strong smelling substances or other food items in the storage place. Eggs stored at 27 to 29 °C for 7 to 10 days will show deterioration changes similar to the same eggs stored at minus 1 °C and 85 percent RH for several months. The changes are due to water loss, carbon dioxide ($CO_2$) and the absorption of volatile odours from the environment.

### *Moisture loss*

Since an egg contains about 74 percent water and the shell is porous, eggs readily lose moisture. A weight loss of 2 to 3 percent is common in marketing and is seldom noticed by the consumer. When losses exceed this level, the air cell is noticeably enlarged by shrinkage in the contents of the egg. This loss is reduced if the storage humidity is high and the temperature is reduced. Coating the eggs with oil and other substances can also reduce the loss. The ideal conditions for egg storage are about minus 1 °C and between 80 to 85 percent RH. At storage temperatures of 10 °C and above, the optimum RH is 80 percent. There is a risk of mould spoilage when the RH is too high. Paper pulp egg trays or other packing materials that readily absorb moisture will accelerate moisture losses from eggs. A temperature as low as 10 °C is unlikely to be practical in rural areas of many developing countries. Temperatures between 10 and 15 °C are more practical, but even then, care should be taken when moving the eggs from cool storage into the outside air with its higher temperature, which often causes condensation to form on the shell, with consequent risks of mould and "rot" growth.

***Microbiological spoilage***

The contents of the egg are usually sterile when the egg is laid. The main cause of contamination is the washing of eggs. Wetting the shell allows micro-organisms on the shell to penetrate and multiply inside. Common indications are green, black and red "rots", mustiness and sourness. The bacteria causing these effects cannot penetrate the shell if it is kept dry. If eggs do become wet through condensation, for example after removal from a cool store into a warmer room, bacteria may then be able to penetrate the shell.

***Tainting***

Eggs, especially yolks, are easily tainted by strong odours, from such sources as disinfectants, soaps, diesel, kerosene, petrol, paint, varnish and wood preservatives. Other foods, such as onions and citrus products, can taint eggs after only a few days of exposure.

## EGG QUALITY CONTROL AND MAINTENANCE

Maintenance of egg quality is a major problem for those involved in egg marketing. The importance of using good packing, storage and transport methods to preserve quality is addressed in other sections below.

Eggs soiled by droppings or the contents of leaking or broken eggs spoil faster than clean eggs. Only good quality eggs should be sent to the market. The simplest way of sorting is to divide the eggs into three categories: cracked, dirty and clean. The cracked eggs should be eaten or sold locally for immediate consumption. The dirty ones should be cleaned and sold locally for consumption within a few days, while the clean eggs can be sent to the major marketing outlet. In some areas, eggs of certain colour or sizes are preferred, and the eggs should be sorted for these qualities.

### Production factors affecting egg quality

The main production factors affecting egg quality are:

- breed and age of the flock;
- type of feed;
- incidence of disease;
- management control of the laying flock; and
- management control of the handling of eggs.

***Breed and age of the laying flock***

The effect of breed on the egg is inherent in many aspects, including the colour, thickness and texture of the shell, the incidence of blood spots, and the amount of thick albumin. While commercial breeders pay constant attention to these factors, there is little that farmers can do to control them.

After the first season of egg production, hens produce eggs of poorer shell quality and poorer egg white thickness, even though the eggs are larger in size. The rate of egg production is also lower. For these reasons as well as the high meat value of the carcass of the older hen in most developing countries, it is advisable to replace the hens after 12 to 18 months of lay.

***Type of feed***

A balanced diet supplied to intensively housed chickens must supply sufficient nutrients to enable the hen to produce an egg with a good shell thickness and good egg yolk colour. A high level of yellow maize, leaf or grass meal will ensure a good yolk colour. Calcium carbonate in some form (limestone or shell) must be supplied (for more detail, see Chapter 3 on Feed Resources and Chapter 4 on General Management). This is either mixed in the ration or fed as a separate supplement on a free-choice basis. It is often quite practicable to have a separate container in a pen with shell or limestone inside.

Fish meal with a high fish oil content fed in the diet can give fishy flavours to eggs produced by hens on those diets.

***Incidence of disease***

The diseases Infectious Bronchitis (IB) and Newcastle Disease both affect egg quality. They cause the hens to lay eggs with misshapen shells and poor quality thick white. IB induces groove-like marks along the long axis of the eggshell.

***Management control over the laying flock***

In many developing countries, there is a belief that a rooster is necessary to stimulate hens to lay. This is not true. The presence of an active male causes the eggs to be laid as fertile eggs (containing an embryo chick), and this reduces the storage stability of the egg. Even after the male is removed, all eggs laid are fertile for up to six weeks because sperm is stored and released from specialised cavities in the hen's oviduct. If fertile eggs are in demand, then cocks should be placed with the hens. Non-fertilized eggs have a much longer shelf life than fertilized eggs and are more suitable for the market.

Dirty eggs can be reduced in number. For hens in deep litter systems, the nest box litter must be clean and replaced regularly. Frequent collection of eggs under any housing management system, and at least four times a day in the hot humid tropics, will reduce the incidence of dirty eggs.

***Management control over egg handling***

## Temperature control

The most effective way to preserve egg quality is to store eggs between 10 and 15 °C during all handling, transport and marketing phases. Insulated containers and/or vehicles can maintain cool temperatures during long-distance transport. Even an outer layer of straw in a basket will help. In hot weather, and where there is no cool storage system, eggs should be transported to market at least every third day. Eggs should never be left standing in the sun or in a very hot room. Air conditioning or even an electric fan is advised whenever practicable. However, as air conditioning has the negative effect of drying out the egg contents as well as the advantageous effect of cooling, wet sacks should be placed as curtains in the cool store to alleviate this dehydrating effect. If fans or air conditioning are not available, then shaded well-ventilated rooms or underground cellars should be used.

## Treatment of dirty eggs

An egg's shell has a natural protective coating (cuticle) that resists the entrance of bacteria and retains moisture inside. Washing eggs with water removes this protection, and thus washed eggs should be eaten as soon as possible. Whether eggs are wet- or dry- cleaned, they should be sold separately from naturally clean eggs, as their storage life is shorter. The cuticle from the shell is a protein-fat substance, and the lack of a cuticle can therefore be detected with a simple ultraviolet (UV) lamp. Washed eggs (without a cuticle) are red in colour under UV-light, while a blue colour indicates that the cuticle is still present.

### *Dry cleaning*

Even with good flock management, some eggs will get dirty. The risks of allowing water to touch the shell have already been mentioned. Dry cleaning systems are preferred. Rubbing lightly with fine sandpaper or a rough cloth is better than wet cleaning. Cloth-backed sandpaper or emery paper can be wrapped around a block of foam rubber for dry cleaning by hand. Steel wool and nylon dishwashing or bathroom scrubbing aids are also quite suitable. Care should be taken not to remove too much of the protective cuticle layer which covers the shell. Only the dirty patches should be cleaned. There are also motor-driven dry-cleaners commercially available. The simplest model consists of a spinning wheel of foam rubber. A mixture of glue and sand is applied periodically to the foam wheel. The operator holds the egg against the spinning foam wheel to clean it.

### *Wet cleaning*

Washing of eggs is only suggested under very well-controlled conditions. The concern is to ensure that the washing water temperature (38 to 43 °C) is never below that of the egg. This avoids the wash water being sucked into the egg through the shell pores by the action of the egg contents shrinking (as happens if the egg is in contact with cooler water). In addition, the washing machine must be able to monitor the detergent/sanitizer/disinfectant/antiseptic levels in the water to ensure that they are optimal. Only special types of non-tainting chemicals can be used. The water itself must be changed frequently. After washing, the shell should be pasteurised by dipping the eggs in water at 82 °C for a few seconds, then dried quickly with warm air before packing. The eggs must also be clearly labelled as "washed". Washing done in this way is complex and expensive, and is therefore only justified in large operations, although even then it involves risks.

## EGG QUALITY GRADING

### Interior quality

#### *Candling*

Opening the egg by breaking it is the only accurate way to fully check the interior quality. This can only be done on a limited sample basis. "Candling" can show some aspects of internal quality without breaking the shell. It consists of inspecting the egg in a beam of light strong enough to penetrate the shell and illuminate the contents. Various types of lamps can be used but the essential features are similar. An incandescent-type bulb of 25 to 50 watts is enclosed in a casing with light exiting through a round hole about 3 cm in diameter against which the egg is held and turned. The casing usually has another hole to provide light for the operator to see the egg container if the room is very dark. By rotating the hand-held egg close to the hole in the candler, the yolk and egg white quality can be estimated by their movement. Experienced operators can candle 24 eggs per minute. The main points to observe are summarised in the following paragraphs.

#### *White*

Egg white (albumin) characteristics showing good egg quality are thick albumin fullness and albumin transparency. When the thick albumin sack is strong and healthy, it is full and confines the yolk within the various layers of egg white. As the thick albumin sack deteriorates, its contents leak into the thin albumin cavity. The yolk then moves more freely, increasing the risk that it might touch the shell and be contaminated by micro-organisms from outside the shell. A healthy albumin is also transparent. It can become discoloured or cloudy due to rot or overexposure to hot water (partial coagulation) in washing.

*Yolk*

Yolk characteristics showing good egg quality are confinement within the thick albumin, a small spherical shape, orange-yellow colour and the absence of spots. As described in the above paragraph, yolk confinement within the albumin protects the yolk from outside contaminants. A small spherical shape indicates a strong yolk membrane. When the egg is exposed to high temperatures and dehydration, the yolk deteriorates and grows larger and flatter. Consumers prefer yolks of orange-yellow colour without spots. Spots on the yolk can indicate: embryo development (reddish colour); blood from the hen's ovary and "meat" bits from the oviduct released during egg formation (red and brown, respectively); moulds (grey or black); or bacterial rots (blue, violet, green or red). Although consumers prefer yolks with no spots, the only spots that pose any health risk are mould and rot spots.

*Air cell*

Air cell characteristics showing good egg quality are small size, shallow depth and fixed position at the blunt end of the egg. Small size and shallow depth indicate very little loss of moisture from the egg contents, which in turn indicates freshness (or that the eggs have been stored under good conditions). A fixed position at the blunt end of the egg indicates that the membranes surrounding the air cell have not been damaged (for example, by rough handling).

There is usually a correlation between the depth of the air cell and other quality aspects. However an egg stored at high temperature and high humidity may show a good air cell depth (as the high humidity maintains the egg moisture) but it may have deteriorated otherwise (as a result of the high temperature).

Air cells can be deflated completely or become unfixed and mobile within the egg. The air cell can become filled with albumin if part of the inner shell membrane is broken. If the membrane is merely weakened, the air cell may move freely around the egg. These mobile air cells are often caused by transporting eggs on rough roads or by the egg being stored small end upwards. The egg could be otherwise quite fresh.

### Shell quality

Before candling, eggshell quality is assessed, and eggs that are dirty, cracked, thin, rough or misshapen are processed accordingly (procedures regarding shell quality are addressed extensively in the above section on production factors affecting egg quality).

## EGG SALE OPTIONS: GRADED SIZE OR TOTAL PACKAGE WEIGHT

Eggs can be sold by graded size or by total package weight. Selling by graded size involves weighing each egg individually and grading the eggs within certain weight ranges (commonly Small, Medium and Large). They are then packed in cartons of 10 or 12 eggs, and sold according to a price per graded size. Selling by total package weight involves packing the eggs without size grading, and selling the package according to a price per kilogram (like almost all other food products).

Consumers in the more developed countries are accustomed to buying eggs graded by size and boxed into cartons. Grading eggs by size requires complex machinery for grading and packaging, as well as monitoring and testing of all grading machines, and sample monitoring of the various grades at retail outlets.

In developing countries without the capital or administrative capacity to undertake such extensive monitoring tasks, the better option is to sell eggs by total package weight. If a market weighing scale is used to weigh foods such as rice or maize, then it can also be used to weigh eggs so that they can be sold by package weight. Selling eggs by package weight also simplifies the situation where standardization of containers and grades has not yet been developed. It also makes price comparisons between different types of food items much easier for the consumer.

Eggs in most developing countries are sold by quantity rather than by weight, which penalizes the producer of larger eggs. As local breeds of hens usually lay uniformly small eggs, this is not a significant problem. However, as the market grows and a demand develops for different sized eggs based on the availability of commercial hybrids (laying larger eggs) in peri-urban areas, the decision to sell eggs by graded size or by total package weight must be faced.

## EGG TRANSPORT

The four concerns regarding egg transport are:

- Protection against **mechanical damage,** which can be achieved by avoiding excessive shaking, especially where roads are bad, and by using spring suspensions on bicycle carriers.
- Protection against **poor egg handling**, which can be achieved by providing convenient loading levels to make lifting easier.
- Protection against **tainting odours.**
- Protection against exposure to **high temperatures** in transport.

### Egg packing methods

Eggs can be packed with a padding of rice husks, wheat chaff or chopped straw in firm-walled baskets or crates. This greatly reduces the risk of shell damage in transport. In Iran, long flat boxes, each containing about 1,000 eggs cushioned in chopped straw, are commonly used for the transport of eggs to the capital from a distance of up to 1 000 km. The boxes are transported in trucks over rough roads, but breakages seldom exceed five percent. The main difficulty with such systems is in standardizing the number of eggs per container. Consignors and receivers will otherwise spend much time counting eggs and repacking to ensure that the correct number has been received for payment.

The standard type of transport egg packing container is the 30-egg tray, which is made of paper pulp holding six rows of five eggs each. The trays are stackable either when full or empty. A standard box of 360 eggs (30 dozen) is made up of two stacks, each comprised of six trays. Washable plastic reusable trays are also available. Cases are usually made of wood. Half-cases to hold 180 eggs (15 dozen) are also common and are usually made of corrugated cardboard.

### Quality preservation during transport

Permissible temperature ranges depend on the duration of transport time. In Europe, the temperature recommendation for two to three day transport in refrigerated vehicles is between -1 °C to 3 °C. In developing countries, however, refrigerated vehicles are not widely available. Even when available, precautions are needed to avoid moisture condensation on eggs removed from the cool container to the warm moist air of the retailing environment.

Fans blowing air towards the eggs across a container of salt and ice is a cooling system that has been used in Pakistan for egg transport by rail for the 1 600 km trip from Peshawar to Karachi, where outside summer temperatures can range from 38 °C to 47 °C.
Refrigerated transport is expensive. In estimating the costs of establishing such a system, the volume of trade for refrigerated goods is an important consideration. The capital cost may be spread over five years to prepare the costing. Transport of other taint-compatible produce with the eggs should be considered; as should the prospect of back-loading with other goods, which may not necessarily require refrigeration.

Public transport such as rail or bus is the most common means of transport in developing countries. Awareness of the special needs for egg transport as addressed above will assist the operator in preserving the quality of the eggs no matter what the type of transport.

## EGG STORAGE

All egg storage systems must meet the following requirements:

- Water loss by evaporation to be minimized.
- Mould and bacteria growth to be minimized.

- Interior quality to be maintained (indicated by a good proportion of a thick white, a firm, rounded yolk and good flavour in both).

The first two requirements can be met (for storage periods of three to five months) by: coating eggs with oil or waterglass (sodium silicate); immersing eggs in limewater (calcium hydroxide solution); or putting eggs in dry storage (using such materials as bran, peat dust, soda lime, salt and wood ash). However, all three of the above requirements can only be met by refrigeration, which is the best storage method, if available.

Following below are descriptions of some of the traditional egg storage methods used in the absence of refrigeration. The first two systems rely on evaporative cooling, which is only effective in the hot dry tropics. The hot humid tropics do not allow sufficient evaporation to occur, and thus there is much less of a cooling effect. Where none of these storage systems can be used, there is no way to slow the inevitable drop in egg quality, and the eggs should therefore be transported to the consumer as quickly as possible.

## Clay pot

Eggs are placed in a clay pot buried in the ground up to its neck, in a shaded area. The pot is covered tightly so that no water gets into the pot. The ground around the pot is watered, but without leaving puddles of water. Straw or a mat is placed in the pot to cushion the eggs and to keep them above any water that seeps into the container. The eggs are put in the pot as soon as they are collected, and covered with a cloth and damp straw. Due to the evaporative cooling effect, the inside of the pot is often five to six Celsius degrees cooler than the outside air temperature. A variation of this method, used in the Sudan, is to bury an earthenware pot in the ground to half its height. A 7 cm layer of mixed sand and clay is packed around the pot up to its neck, and kept wet by sprinkling water on it. The inside of the pot is lined with grass. The eggs inside are covered with a thin cloth to allow air circulation. Evaporative cooling in Sudan's hot dry climate often reduces the egg temperature to up to eight-Celsius degrees below that of the air outside. Eggs are turned daily to prevent the yolks touching the shell, which would accelerate the decaying process.

### Wet sack cooler

This is another method utilising the evaporative cooling principle. The sack material is kept wet by having a tray of water above the hanging sack, into which the neck-edge of the sack material is dipped, keeping the sack wet. A slightly more sophisticated system uses perforated pipes connected to a water tank. To prevent mould formation, the sacking is pre-soaked in a solution of copper sulphate ($CuSO_4$), using 60 g of crystals in four litres of water.

## Oil coating

A thin film of oil on an eggshell fills its pores and reduces evaporation and thus spoilage of the egg contents. Using a wire basket, the eggs are dipped into slightly heated oil, about 11 °C warmer than the eggs. Special odourless, colourless, low viscosity mineral oils can be used. If these are not available, then any light mineral oil or almost any cooking oil that doesn't easily turn rancid serves the purpose. To reuse the oil, it is cleaned through a filter and heated to 116 °C to sterilize it. Four litres of oil coats about 7,000 eggs. Oiled eggs last for at least three weeks (longer if kept at 10 °C, or less at temperatures above 21 °C). For high temperature storage, eggs should be oiled four to six hours after laying.

## Waterglass paste

Waterglass is a paste or ointment of sodium silicate in water. It is rubbed onto the hands and then the egg is rolled between the two waterglass-coated hands to transfer a waterproof coating of waterglass paste to the eggshell.

### Waterglass solution

For 100 eggs, a 25-litre pot or jar is used, and 5.3 litres of previously boiled (and then cooled) water are mixed with 0.5 litres of waterglass. The eggs are placed in the pot and covered with the waterglass solution. The pot is covered and kept in a cool, shaded place. The eggs keep for one to six months.

### Limewater solution

Limewater is a solution of calcium hydroxide [$Ca(OH)_2$], a mild alkali. The main ingredient is burnt lime (also known as quicklime). The chemical name of this is calcium oxide (CaO). It is also known as *choon* in Bangladesh, and is a common ingredient of the betel nut mixture chewed by people in many tropical countries. Calcium oxide is made by burning limestone ($CaCO_3$) in a hot fire. Carbon dioxide ($CO_2$) is driven off from the limestone, leaving CaO behind as a white powder. Dissolving this calcium oxide in water makes limewater. The resultant solution of calcium hydroxide is only partly soluble, and the insoluble portion will settle to the bottom of the container.

Six litres of limewater is made by stirring 2.3 kg of calcium oxide into six litres of boiled (then cooled) water. It is allowed to stand overnight so that the insoluble portion settles. The eggs and the clear part of the limewater solution are placed in a pot, covered and kept cool. The eggs last more than a month. In the years prior to 1970, eggs were commonly transported from Bangladesh (formerly East Pakistan) to Pakistan (formerly West Pakistan) on a train journey of about a month, in high temperatures. The eggs were stored in earthenware jars containing limewater and maintained their quality well.

### Hot water immersion

Immersion in hot water for carefully controlled lengths of time has a pasteurizing effect, which kills the embryo in fertile eggs, destroys some of the bacteria on the shell and stabilizes the quality of the egg white. The difficulty is to achieve this without coagulating some of the egg white. Equivalent effects are achieved with any of the following temperature-time combinations:

| | |
|---|---|
| 35 minutes at | 49 °C |
| 15 | 54 °C |
| 10 | 59 °C |
| 5 | 60 °C |

This method requires special equipment and supervision.

### Salt and wet clay or ashes

Eggs are coated in a mixture of salt and wet clay or ashes which allows them to keep for one month. This method has been practised for centuries in China.

### Cooked rice and salt

Eggs are covered with a mixture of cooked rice and salt, which allows them to keep for six months. This method has been practised for centuries in China.

### Lime, salt, wood ashes and tea

Eggs are covered with a layer of lime, salt and wood ashes mixed with a tea infusion, which allows them to keep for several years. This method has been practised for centuries in China.

# Chapter 10
# Research and Development for Family Poultry

Research and development in the field of Family Poultry (FP) must first examine the social, cultural and technical constraints faced by this sector, and then observe how these have been addressed in past efforts and whether the lessons are being applied in currently ongoing efforts. While holding this perspective, the need for further research, training and extension must then be assessed in the light of a clear understanding of what the overall development objectives are, and what place FP has in achieving them. Having provided background in the preceding nine chapters, this final chapter takes the reader through these concluding stages.

## SOCIO-CULTURAL CONSTRAINTS TO DEVELOPMENT

A sociological appraisal is essential in determining strategies for development. Technical and economic appraisals are also necessary, but are insufficient on their own. Socio-cultural factors contribute to the wide variety of response of livestock keepers even under identical economic conditions. Many socio-cultural factors affect livestock production. For example, some communities ban ducks, as they are presumed dirty and destructive to drinking water supplies. Some communities regard pigeons as a sign of peace and concord. In such communities, the presence of pigeons is regarded as a good omen, and their departure would presage disaster. In other communities, pigeons are regarded as an evil omen, since they are used by native doctors in sinister rituals.

Another socio-cultural constraint to poultry development is the value placed upon poultry for use at ceremonies and festivals or even as a source of income in times of need but not as a source of daily food nor as a regular source of income. Some regard chickens as their pets or part of the family, thus it is only the arrival of an important unexpected visitor that could allow their use as food, although they can be sold without regret and the money utilised.

Another major constraint to poultry production is the high value placed upon crop production rather than livestock production. This affects the willingness to put much time, expense and effort into livestock production. Theft is also a great constraint. Villagers who have lost all their poultry to theft may be reluctant to face the expense of starting again.

Another constraint is the social norm that determines ownership of livestock. Typically, where crop farming is the men's main activity, keeping livestock is perceived as a peripheral activity relegated to women and children. However, when the number of livestock increases, men usually take over the activity.

It should not be assumed that socio-cultural factors can be changed. However, by incorporating socio-cultural factors into development strategies, the programmes and technologies may encounter less resistance. Development programmes, which combine local knowledge with western science, yield strategies which are culturally more acceptable. Socio-cultural factors are thus not seen as a problem, but rather as a factor to be considered or used in finding a solution (Olawoye and di Domenico, 1990).

## TECHNICAL CONSTRAINTS TO DEVELOPMENT

The most common FP flock size of between 5 to 20 birds seems to be the limit that can be kept by a family without special inputs in terms of feeding, housing and labour. These small flocks scavenge sufficient feed in the surroundings of the homestead to survive and to reproduce. Any significant increase in flock size often leads to malnutrition if no feed supplement is provided. In addition, larger flock sizes must forage at greater distances, which may involve damage to neighbours' vegetable gardens. Any move to fence in or enclose the poultry then involves the need to provide a balanced ration. Larger flock sizes can easily arise once mortality is reduced through vaccination and improved hygiene. Flock size can rapidly increase to the point where the feed requirement exceeds the available Scavengable Feed Resource Base (SFRB) in the area around the dwelling (For more detail on the SFRB concept, see Chapter 3 "Feed Resources"). At this stage, either supplementary feeding or a semi-intensive system of management is required. If balanced feed, day-old hybrid chick and vaccine input supplies (and markets) are available and well organized, and then intensive poultry management systems may be a viable option. There have been many attempts to take short cuts to development and to start immediately with the semi-intensive system.

## FAO consultation 1987

A wide range of approaches to improve FP production has been tried. An FAO Expert Consultation on Rural Poultry Development in Asia was held in Bangladesh in March 1987, to review these approaches in order to identify the reasons for success or failure. A major issue during the workshop was to clearly define the different systems of rural poultry production. There was confusion in terminology between the low-technology scavenging systems of Bangladesh, Myanmar and Bhutan, and the small semi-intensive or intensive production systems (a few hundred birds) kept in India, Malaysia and Indonesia.

**Table 10.1** The effect of rural poultry improvement on production, reproduction and off-take per hen/year

| Production system | Nº of eggs/hen/year | Nº of year-old chickens | Nº of eggs for consumption and sale |
|---|---|---|---|
| **Traditional** | 20 – 30 | 2 - 3 | 0 |
| Step 0: Scavenging: no regular water or feed, poor night shelter | | | |
| **Improved Traditional** | 40 – 60 | 4 - 8 | 10 - 20 |
| Step 1: offered water and supplementary feed, improved shelter, care in first weeks, ND vaccination | | | |
| Step 2: as in step 1 plus further feeding, watering, housing; treatment for parasites, additional vaccinations | 100 | 10 - 12 | 30 - 50 |
| Step 3: (semi-intensive) as in step 2 with improved breeds and complete diets | 160 – 180 | 25 - 30 | 50 - 60 |

Source: Bessei, 1987

These differences motivated the FAO consultation facilitator (Bessei, 1987) to classify the various poultry production systems in Asia (Table 10.1, above). The table shows the logical evolution from Step 0 to Step 3, and the Consultation agreed that many development projects had failed because they did not recognise the constraints present at the different steps of development. The constraints themselves (shown in Table 10.2) show the need for awareness raising in the farmers to recognise the needs of their poultry for regular watering and feeding, cleaning of the poultry night house and care of the young chicks. The Consultation recommended that the first critical step for rural poultry development is the encouragement and support of farmers to change their traditional system. Taking into consideration the chronic shortages of personnel and transport affecting extension services in the developing countries, the Consultation emphasized the importance of selecting pilot farms to serve as models as they can have a multiplier effect on the neighbouring farms and villages.

Perhaps because of the variety of understandings of rural poultry development, many of the methods suggested seem more suited to the development of small units of intensive poultry production. The methods reflect the procedures required for transfer of new technology or total replacement of existing practices. For instance, incentives were required to encourage farmers to participate in the programmes, perhaps indicating that the programmes were not consistent with the priorities of the farmers. Selection of farmers was also identified as a major factor in determining the success or failure of a development programme. Incentives can often lead to the selection of farmers not genuinely interested in poultry production. To ensure the selection of authentic candidates, the following procedure was recommended:

- The extension service should select farmers already known to be particularly interested in poultry production.
- Incentives should never be given in cash.
- Incentives should always be associated with certain commitments by the farmers (for example, equipment for poultry houses should be provided only if the farmer has constructed the poultry shed at his own cost).
- Supplies of inputs such as day-old chicks, fertile eggs, feed and vaccines should be made at cost price.

The pilot farm method risks failure if a large amount of foreign input (such as equipment and construction materials) is needed to establish it because neighbouring farms can become discouraged by the fact that they are unable to procure the same equipment.

**Table 10.2** Technical constraints and training requirements for family poultry development

| Constraint | Training Measures required |
|---|---|
| Disease risk | Advice on sanitation and health; training vaccinators. |
| Predators | Advice on predator control. |
| Housing | Advice on improved poultry housing. |
| Feed and water | Advice on locally available feed ingredients and their combinations; making of feeders and drinkers; regular provision of feed and water. |
| Genetic potential | Introduction of improved indigenous (and if necessary, exotic) breeds and advice on special management. |
| Marketing | Advice on egg handling and storage, and training of farmers in group management and marketing. |

Source: Bessei, 1987

In order to be effective in the process of technology and information transfer, pilot farms should be charged with special duties, which bring them obligatorily in contact with the other poultry keepers. Pilot poultry farmers have been successfully trained in Bangladesh and Burkina Faso to vaccinate chickens and guinea fowls, respectively. Pilot farmers can also be used to provide improved lines or to raise pullets for distribution so that a number of farms in the surrounding area will be regularly served with inputs and information.

Attempts to by-pass the phases as described by Bessei (1987) usually fail, and it appears that the transitory phases (especially Steps 1 and 2 as described in Table 10.1) are important if the development is starting from the traditional scavenging system. It has been noted that even in successful poultry development programmes, the supply of feed and veterinary products often lags behind the increase in flock size, especially if it is organized by the government extension service. The use of non-governmental organizations (NGOs) and private entrepreneurs is a better alternative.

## INFPD and the 1998 FAO e-conference

The International Network for Family Poultry Development (INFPD) started as the African Network for Rural Poultry Development (ANRPD), and was established during an international workshop on rural poultry development held in November 1989 in Ile-Ife, Nigeria. The name was changed to INFPD at a meeting that took place in M'Bour, Senegal, in December 1997 (Sonaiya, 2000). INFPD is mainly an information exchange network. One of its objectives is to encourage higher standards of research and development that can sustainably increase the productivity of the FP subsector. This is achieved through providing advice and collecting data and detailed information about FP production systems. Information is disseminated through a trilingual (English, French and Spanish) newsletter, produced twice yearly and distributed electronically (with a printed version for members without email facilities) with the assistance of FAO.

In December 1998, FAO held the first INFPD/FAO electronic conference on FP, which proved so popular and interactive that it was extended until July 1999. The introductory paper to this conference addressed the issue of research and development options for FP (Sonaiya *e. al.*, 1999). The layout of this important introductory paper was:

- Research options for family poultry development.
- Prospects for development.
- Development approaches.
- Breeding and reproduction (evaluation and selection of indigenous breeds).
- Evaluation and adaptation of imported breeds to hot climates.
- Feed research and development.
- Health management.
- Entrepreneur development.
- Information management.

All papers, comments and discussions are available on the FAO/INFPD website. The constraints and issues facing FP that were recognized by the e-conference are:

## Disease

Newcastle disease (ND) constitutes the most serious epizootic poultry disease in the world, particularly in developing countries. No progress has been made in controlling ND in free-ranging village flocks, which represent more than 80 percent of the total poultry population. Several recent surveys in Africa showed high rates of seropositivity in the absence of vaccination. In developing countries, ND occurs every year and kills an average of 70 to 80 percent of the unvaccinated village hens (Branckaert *et al.*, 2000). It is very difficult to organize vaccination campaigns covering free-range birds. The main constraints are:

- the difficulty of grouping together an adequately large number of birds in order to obtain an efficient vaccination rate;
- the possibility of disease cross-contamination arising from birds of various ages being raised together; and
- the difficulty of maintaining an efficient cold chain for proper vaccine quality preservation.

Diseases make poultry production a risky venture. FP producers using the free-range extensive system acknowledge this risk, and reduce its impact on the household economy by having small flocks. ND is a major disease problem for all FP producers wherever the disease exists. Vaccination of the flock against ND is very important and provides a basis for further development.

It is worth repeating that the reluctance of farmers to invest in poultry production is not due to a lack of resources but to the risk of disease outbreaks and mortality. Killer diseases like ND regularly decimate village flocks. In traditional farming systems, farmers often live close to the survival limit, so they naturally avoid risks. Minimizing risk ranks higher than increasing output. A key component of FP development is the control of the most important diseases. Regular vaccination is a prerequisite for any improvement in FP production.

Although the control of ND is the key constraint, there are other disease constraints, which rise in importance as soon as higher-ranking constraints are eliminated. Many poultry development projects have failed because only one constraint was tackled or, when more than one constraint was considered, the importance of other problems was poorly understood. Many projects concentrated either on disease control or on genetic improvement. There is no doubt that vaccination reduces mortality, but in one particular project, in certain periods, mortality due to predation was as high as 70 percent and the effect of vaccination was further negated by a secondary constraint of poor housing (Bourzat and Saunders, 1987). Generally, the costs of an isolated vaccination campaign cannot be justified unless actions to improve housing and feeding are also taken.

## Predators

Predators such as snakes, rats, dogs, cats, foxes, racoons and birds of prey represent the main causes of predator losses, especially in young birds. Human beings can also represent another important predator for adult birds. Proper shelter should be constructed using locally available materials, and predators should be trapped, hunted or repelled by specific plants (Branckaert *e. al.,* 2000). For example, in Nigeria, sliced garlic (*Allium sativum*) is placed around poultry houses to repel snakes.

Analysis of mortality in FP flocks in Thailand (Thitisak, 1992) showed that the first four months of life are critical for the growing chicks. The mortality of chicks during this period often rose to 60 percent (Matthewman, 1977) even in flocks vaccinated for ND. In Africa, while various other diseases such as Salmonellosis or coccidiosis affected the chicks during the first two months of age (Chabeuf, 1990), the most important cause of mortality between two and four months of age was predation, by dogs, cats, hawks and snakes, which caused up to 70 percent mortality (Bourzat and Saunders, 1987). Overnight housing is an important way to reduce this loss, and can utilize locally available materials of reasonable cost.

## Feeding

Feed is also an input of major concern and the supply of adequate feed supplement is critical. The nutrient intake of scavenging birds varies from place to place according to the seasons, the crops grown and the natural vegetation available. In field experiments, feed supplements, including household waste (cooked potatoes, yams or cassava tubers), and oilseed cakes, have a positive effect on egg production and body weight of scavenging birds.

Careful attention should be given to ensuring adequate feed resources. Feed represents 60 to 80 percent of the input cost in the intensive commercial poultry sector. In Low Income, Food-Deficient Countries (LIFDCs), a surplus of cereals is generally not available. It is therefore not advisable to develop a wholly grain-based feeding system. The recommended policy is to identify and use locally available feed resources to formulate diets that are as balanced as possible (Branckaert . *et al.,* 2000).

Full *ad libitum* feeding of a balanced ration is essential for poultry intensively managed in confinement, even on a small scale. The usual recommendation is for commercially manufactured feed, but many farmers find it too costly and not in regular supply. The by-products of processing of local crops (brans, and oil and seed cakes) can be used as both energy and protein sources (see Chapter 3 "Feed Resources") but on their own cannot make a balanced ration. More research is needed on local feed resources as sources of trace elements, minerals and vitamins, especially from leaves, fruits, algae, fungi and other available materials. However, even with this knowledge, the skills of a well-equipped and experienced nutritionist are needed to formulate least-cost balanced rations.

## Breeding (genetic potential)

Indigenous or local breeds are generally raised in FP production systems. These birds are exposed to natural selection from the environment for hardiness, running and flight skills, but not for egg production. Hens are thus poor layers, but good mothers (except for guinea hens). When farmers contemplate the adoption of a more intensive poultry production system, they are eager to purchase more productive birds. There is a need to find the best method to provide them with such birds, and the options are:

- to supply hybrid strains, which requires the presence of well-managed hatchery facilities and (grand) parent stock, or
- to supply pure-bred breeds, which allows the farmer to renew his flock and to remain independent from external suppliers. Unfortunately, pure-bred breeds are becoming more difficult and more expensive to purchase, and produce fewer eggs than hybrids. (Branckaert *et al.,* 2000).

Genetic improvement has been considered a high priority in poultry development projects. Usually vaccination programmes are carried out during genetic upgrading programmes, but feed supply to the improved birds has not received sufficient attention. Thus it has not been possible to exploit the superior genetic potential of the improved birds.

## Marketing

Poultry products in most developing countries, especially in Africa, are still expensive. The marketing system is generally informal and poorly developed. Unlike eggs and meat from commercial hybrid birds (derived from imported stock), local consumers generally prefer those from indigenous stocks. The existence of a local market offering good sales opportunities and adequate transport facilities are obvious prerequisites for FP development. As most consumers with greater purchasing power live in and around cities, intensification of poultry production should be initiated in peri-urban areas or, at least, in areas having a good road network (Branckaert *et al.,* 2000).

Traditional dealers and middlemen, who collect eggs and birds from the villages, facilitate the marketing of FP products in most developing countries. Such traditional marketing structures are often overlooked, bypassed or criticised. There has been a regrettable tendency in some countries to use government extension services or parastatals to market family poultry products. This practice should be discouraged as it is not sustainable.

## Farmer organizations

Organizing FP farmers is not an easy task, for several reasons. Flock sizes are small and birds are maintained with minimal land, labour and capital inputs. Thus farmers generally consider FP a secondary activity compared with other agricultural activities. Nevertheless, it is essential to develop producer groups, which give members easier access to essential inputs (such as feed, improved breeds, medicine, vaccines and technical advice) and to credit, training, transportation and the marketing of poultry products. Producer groups also encourage more educated people to initiate FP farming as a secondary activity (conducted at the family level using medium-sized flocks), as well as facilitating the development of associated activities such as market gardening, which can utilize poultry manure and help to reduce or remove household waste and pests (Branckaert *et al.,* 2000).

Farmers should be allowed to develop the market structures most suitable for them. Often women's groups prove to be effective in marketing eggs along with other products at local markets. Such groups should be encouraged and supported if they exist, but their establishment solely for FP may be unnecessary and unviable.

In a case study in the region of Niamey, Niger (Kobling, 1989), it was shown that smallholdings (less than 20 hens) of layers, which were situated beyond 2.5 km from a main paved road, could supply eggs and meat to the city market at competitive prices. Villages much farther from the main routes could supply live birds competitively but not eggs. Eggs are not an important food item at the village level, as it is a relatively high-priced protein food, and thus marketing may require cooperative efforts by producers to transport eggs to larger towns. Possibilities for this include using existing commercial trading channels or opening new channels such as those through producer associations, cooperatives, women's groups or young farmer associations. The establishment of specialized poultry production cooperatives has proved difficult in many places, and socio-economic factors play an important part in this.

### Training and management

As was emphasized at the beginning of this chapter by Bessei (1987), technical skills need to be considered at both farmer and extension officer levels. Training is essential in the areas of disease control, housing, equipment, feeding, genetic improvement and marketing. A basic knowledge of specific features of poultry anatomy and physiology is also important, to provide a basis for understanding the above topics. Housing and management could be improved through appropriate farmer training, preferably conducted on-farm. Local craftsmen could be trained to manufacture small equipment, such as feeders and drinkers (Branckaert *et al.*, 2000).

## RESEARCH LESSONS LEARNED FROM COMPLETED PROJECTS

### Genetic upgrading

This was the earliest and most commonly favoured FP development strategy, and has been adopted and supported by many donors from the 1960s onwards. It has usually involved substantial investment in government infrastructure (in terms of establishing farms and buildings to multiply stock numbers), and less investment in training village farmers or developing distribution networks for vaccine and medicine. The Cockerel Exchange Programme (CEP) represented the traditional approach, in which cockerels from exotic strains were reared up to 15 to 20 weeks of age, usually in government poultry farms, and then exchanged with local cockerels owned by FP households, which kept small flocks and were requested to remove or exchange all local cockerels. In addition, sometimes the flocks of the farmers (or of the whole village), were vaccinated against ND, and the farmers were given advice on poultry feeding and housing.

In the Machakos district of Kenya, an evaluation by Ballard (1985, as cited in Mbugua, 1990) of the performance of hens upgraded through a CEP in 1977 (using a layer hybrid strain cockerel) showed an increase in egg production of about 30 eggs per hen in a flock of nine hens and one cock (Table 10.3).

**Table 10.3** Production increase per hen of a nine-hen flock in Kenya

| Per hen, per year | Local hens (before) | Improved hens (after) |
|---|---|---|
| Eggs per hen | 57 | 87 |
| Eggs for consumption and sale | 41 | 63 |
| Eggs for hatching | 16 | 24 |
| Chicks hatched | 11 | 17 |
| Birds for consumption and sale | 3.2 | 4.9 |

Source: Ballard, 1985 (as cited in Mbuga, 1990)

The CEP method is criticised mainly because the raising of cockerels in government farms is costly, and exposure of the intensively raised cockerels to village conditions leads to considerable adaptation problems with resulting mortalities of 50 percent or more. Also, local cockerels are not always removed, as the farmer (quite rightly in many cases) distrusts the survival and mating ability of the exotic cockerel. The presence of the local cocks reduces the effectiveness of the attempt at genetic improvement, as they are easily able to compete for the favours of the local hens against the exotic breed cocks.

In view of the problems of the CEP, other methods have been developed, including the distribution of chicks, pullets and hatching eggs of improved breeds. A comparison of the relative efficiency of these upgrading methods (ter Horst, 1987), based on the number of "improved" day-old chicks produced in the village over three years, showed that the distribution of hatching eggs was the most cost-effective method (as shown in Table 10.4 below).

**Table 10.4** Efficiency of strategies for improving poultry production

| Strategy | Percent increase |
|---|---|
| Distribution of pullets | 15 |
| Exchange of cockerels | 17 |
| Distribution of day-old chicks | 67 |
| Distribution of hatching eggs | 100 |

Source: ter Horst, 1987.

In operation, hatching eggs of selected lines are sold to families raising poultry. Local broody hens hatch the eggs. The chicks are raised by the hens and adapt easily to the environment. The distribution of hatching eggs is thus the least costly and most efficient method of genetic upgrading. This method has the following advantages and disadvantages.

**Advantages** of distributing hatching eggs:

- The eggs represent a low project cost, compared with pullets or cockerels.
- The eggs convey 100 percent of genetic improvement, compared with cockerels or pullets, which contribute only 50 percent when crossed with local birds.
- The young chicks are raised under natural conditions from day-old age, and develop or learn scavenging ability.

**Disadvantages** of distributing hatching eggs:

- Cockerels are generally more appreciated and accepted by the poultry farmers. This hampers the introduction of improved breeds through distribution of hatching eggs in the same area.
- Transport of hatching eggs under rough conditions and with unsuitable packaging reduces hatchability.
- The total replacement of local chickens by improved birds of exotic origin leads to: a loss of biodiversity of the local poultry population; a loss of brooding and hatching ability in the hen; and a breakdown of the self-sustained system of reproduction at the village level. These are serious problems and must also be considered.

The words that follow come from a prominent Nigerian livestock expert, (Suleiman, 1990), but they reflect the growing appreciation of the genetic and environmental resources placed in the care of all people of all countries: "Perhaps the time has come for us to redefine the ideology for the development of African agriculture and indeed the entire economy. African agricultural ideology appears to be based on the premise that the genetic resources indigenous to the continent are inferior to those found elsewhere and as such they must be replaced or diluted to a large extent by genetic materials foreign to the continent. Similarly, we have viewed our environment as hostile and, in fact, a direct threat to our existence. These postures have prevented us from capitalising on the strengths of our genetic and environmental resource endowments. We must move from a position of emphasizing the weaknesses of our resource endowments to one of amplifying their positive aspects, while seeking to overcome the weaknesses inherent in them."

### Vaccination

Protection against Newcastle Disease requires three vaccinations during the six-month growing phase of pullets and cockerels. Depending on local conditions, between two and three vaccinations per year are needed for adult birds. Because of the limited resources of government veterinary services, it is necessary to build networks of private veterinarians, veterinary assistants and vaccinators to provide preventive veterinary care in remote rural areas, and to ensure a reliable supply of vaccines (with a cold chain for the storage and distribution of conventional vaccines). In Bangladesh, the Department of Livestock Services established such a cold chain from the vaccine production laboratory to the village level in 1984. Within three years, 4 500 poultry farmers (especially women) were trained as village poultry vaccinators. The full cost of vaccination was charged to poultry producers in order to sustain the full cost of vaccine production and distribution. When it is possible to extend this fee to partly cover an extension service, it can result in the creation of a partly privatised poultry extension service. Such a system, financed by vaccination fees and the sale of exotic birds to farmers, was established in Sao Tome and Principe.

### Strategy combinations

A combined approach, including vaccination against ND, the provision of a regular water supply and feed supplements (household waste) and special care for the young chicks during the first weeks of life (for example, through improved night shelters and creep feeders), increases the number of eggs laid by about 100 percent as well as increasing the number of chickens raised per hen/year to between 10 and 12.

The introduction of genetic improvement, in combination with further improvement in feeding (compound feed), housing (semi-confinement) and health (full vaccination and anti-parasites), will again increase egg production by approximately 50 percent and egg weight by 60 percent.

## RESEARCH LESSONS LEARNED FROM CURRENT PROJECTS

Some countries have had successes in developing FP systems. In Egypt, the *Fayoumi* District Cooperative has raised the productivity and incomes of village FP producers. It distributes improved *Fayoumi* local birds and produces supplementary feed at its own feed mill using mostly local ingredients. It also assists farmers in marketing their eggs and birds.

In Malaysia, small flocks of poultry are fed on "Domestic Feed", a reduced-price feed marketed by feed millers with a lower "nutrient density" (balanced for all nutrients, but lower in energy because of the inclusion of low-energy ingredients such as rice or wheat bran) than commercial broiler diets. In 1986, village egg and poultry meat production in Malaysia was estimated at 150 million eggs and 17,000 tonnes of meat, accounting for five percent of total egg production and seven percent of total poultry meat. Due to a high demand for village poultry meat, some of the backyard village poultry flocks have evolved into relatively large-scale commercial village chicken producers. Some of these farms rear between 2 000 and 15 000 young stock, which are then sold for growing under the traditional extensive system.

In Uganda, duck meat production rose from 600 to 3,500 tonnes in the 12 years between 1980 and 1992. This was achieved by improving health care in the traditional small-scale FP units, with the result that average mortality decreased from over 40 percent in 1980 to less than eight percent in 1994 (Country Profile 1994).

### The Bangladesh model (FAO e-conference 2002) and research topics

In Bangladesh, there has been a significant effort over the past 20 years to develop the FP system. The Bangladesh model was the subject of the second FAO/INFPD electronic conference on FP "The Bangladesh model and other experiences in FP development", which was held in May-July 2002. All papers, comments and discussions were compiled and presented on the

FAO/INFPD website (http://www.fao.org/ag/aga/AGAP/LPA/ fampo1/fampo.htm.) within two months of the conference conclusion.

What was not covered in the e-conference about the Bangladesh situation was more detail on their views on research priorities and what progress they have made. Bangladesh determined five areas for research potential in FP:

- disease;
- feeding;
- breeding;
- marketing and socio-economics; and,
- management and production.

These are close to the same categories outlined above under the Technical Constraints section. Under the above five headings, the Bangladesh Department of Livestock Services poultry research committee suggested protocol outlines for research proposals in FP (those marked below with an asterisk were regarded as being of top priority as of October 2000), under the Bangladesh government's poultry model FP improvement programme, which is currently (1998-2005) aided by the Asian Development Bank and Danida in two ongoing overlapping projects.

The protocol outlines were intended as guidance for formulating detailed research proposals or study proposals for post-graduate degrees or activities of research institutions or NGOs. The protocol outlines are detailed below:

***Disease***

- Disease prevalence study (epidemiology):
  - host bird (age, sex and breed);
  - morbidity and mortality;
  - management and feeding;
  - spatial and temporal factors;
  - parasitism and feed consumption efficiency; and
  - vaccine and vaccination failure.
- In-depth study of major serious diseases:
  - identification, characterization and virulence of the causal agent;
  - serological characterization; and
  - pathogenicity.
- Development of a disease-control strategy based on vaccination:
  - vaccination schedule;
  - maternal antibody and its effects on immunization; and
  - establishment of diagnostic networks.
- Development and improvement of vaccination:
  - development of vaccine types using local vaccine;
  - comparative study of local and imported vaccines;
  - comparing of heat tolerance selection in present ND vaccines with the use of I2 or V4 strains; and
  - use of heat-tolerant ND I2 seed vaccine produced in district veterinary laboratories using eggs from the same district.
- Study of disease prevalence in different locations and the seasonal effect of these on different breeds and breed combinations.
- Study of the quantification of semi-scavenger losses associated with the main diseases, including possible remedial measures against these diseases.

***Feeding***

- Study of the possibilities of protein banks, and the cultivation of Ipil-ipil (*Leucaena)*, duckweed and snails at the smallholder FP level.
- Study of year-round nutrient availability for scavenging chicken under model key rearer conditions.
- Study of year-round protein production from various conventional and unconventional resources:
  - manure-based duckweed production in shallow ponds with clean and polluted water sources;
  - protein supply from leaves, such as cassava, *Leucaena, Sesbania,* and *Glyrecidia;* and
  - animal protein supply, for example from blood meal, rumen microbes, earthworms, insects, hatchery by-product waste, and leather by-products.
- Study and nutritional evaluation of various feed ingredients used for feeding poultry under semi-scavenging conditions:
  - chemical composition;
  - nutritive value from feeding trials; and
  - preservation of feedstuffs.
- Study of the effective optimum level of supplementation for semi-scavenging birds in different agro-ecological conditions, for all age groups of birds:
  - effect of supplementing protein meal (vegetable and animal protein);
  - effect of supplementing energy-rich feed (both conventional and unconventional); and
  - effect of supplementing minerals with ingredients (both conventional and unconventional).
- Nutrient recycling through manure-based protein production under semi-scavenging conditions:
  - energy flow of the FP farm (conventional and improved systems); and
  - protein economy (traditional FP and improved systems).
- Study of how much and what combination of feed ingredients is most economical as a feed for Model Key Rearers in different environments, seasons and regions.
- Study of the utilization of non-conventional feed ingredients, such as tealeaf waste, duckweed, poultry litter, earthworms and insects (cultivated and natural), as protein sources for semi-scavenging poultry.
- Study of the amount and composition of available feeds for scavenging and their seasonal and regional variations.
- Study of the available Scavenger Feed Resource Base and the optimum chicken number density for sustainable semi-scavenging in the FP rearing system under Bangladesh socio-economic conditions.
- Comparison of crop-contents and feed weigh-back systems using the cafeteria system of feed supplementation.
- Study of whether the cultivation of such chicken feed as earthworms, maggots, termites and cockroaches can be incorporated within the FP small-scale livestock development (SLD) system.
- Study of how industrial by-products such as those from breweries and fish processing plants can be used as supplementary feed for the semi-scavenging FP model.

***Breeding***

- Comparative profitability studies between: two commercial cross-breeds (locally marketed as *Harco* and *Nera,* both derived by crossing Rhode Island Red (RIR) and Barred

Plymouth Rock [BPR]); and also between the locally bred *Sonali* (RIR and *Fayoumi*); and pure "local" *Fayoumi* (an Egyptian breed multiplied in Bangladesh without artificial selection pressure, in confinement management conditions for the past 20 years); under both FP traditional scavenging and FP semi-scavenging (feed supplemented) systems.

- According to previous studies and research, the *Sonali* was found to be superior in terms of meat and egg production, disease resistance and overall profitability in both the FP traditional scavenging and semi-scavenging systems. This research was undertaken by the Department of Livestock Services, the Bangladesh Livestock Research Institute (BLRI) (both supported by the now-completed Danida-assisted Small-scale Livestock Development project [SLDP-1], and the Bangladesh Agricultural University (BAU). Further study is planned to determine what type of selection index should be applied to the parent stocks, and under what type of environment, in order to improve its efficiency and performance under the semi-scavenging system. The parent stocks are the *Fayoumi* and RIR. This is related to a protocol suggested in the Marketing and Socio-economics category below.
- Crossing of dominant Naked-Neck breeds with *Fayoumi* or RIR for higher egg production and meat production, disease resistance and profitability in scavenging and semi-scavenging systems.
- Crossing of Naked-Neck breeds with *desi* (local indigenous breeds), for increasing both size and brooding capacity.
- Development and maintenance of grandparent stock, to maintain the breeding efficiency of RIR and *Fayoumi*.
- Study of the performance of different breed combinations under various environments, feeds and disease situations.
- Conducting of stock density trials of different breeds and breed combinations, to determine the optimum FP flock size for best productivity.
- Comparing the performance of commercial breeds with the *desi* and other "home-made combinations" made by Key Rearers, using broody hens under FP traditional and semi-scavenging systems.

***Marketing and Socio-economics***

- Study of the impact of the Participatory Livestock Development project (PLDP) activities (expected duration 1998-2003) on income generation, employment and poverty in rural Bangladesh.
- Study of the impact of the SLDP concept on the nutritional health of women and young girls at the village level. An M.Sc. study on this subject has already been completed by a post-graduate student of the Royal Veterinary and Agricultural University (KVL), Denmark (Nielsen, 2000).
- Study of the nutritional status and effect on work capacity, as well as body mass ratios of both mother and children, in households using the FP semi-scavenger system, compared with those using the traditional FP system.
- Comparative cost and returns analysis of poultry production under the scavenging and confinement poultry farming systems.
- Study of the changing role of women in livestock rearing under PLDP.
- Study of the demand and supply of poultry products, identifying the constraints to successful market operations.
- Study of the development of market intermediaries (middlemen) and their constraints in the project areas.
- Study of the effect of NGO modes of operation on the participation in and extension of poultry model practices.

- Study of the socio-economic impact of smallholder poultry production when combined with such other activities as vegetable production and fish-culture.
- Comparative studies of the economy of egg and meat production between the scavenging and commercial systems. Examination of the economics of raising cockerels of *Fayoumi* and *Sonali* at the village level.
- Assessment of the extent to which PLDP and SLDP-1 were able to address the "gender gaps" in the socio-economic situation of Bangladesh, as well as determining how and where earnings from poultry were spent (for example, in social, health or education areas).
- Study of the actual rate of interest faced by the beneficiaries of the various Poultry Model enterprises, and by the different NGOs partnered in PLDP.

***Management and production***

- Economic use of home-made heaters and fuels for artificial brooding and incubating systems.
- Determination of the optimum construction and design of a suitable low-cost brooder-rearing house, using the raised slatted bamboo floor (*macha*) system. Use of materials of various types, thicknesses and costs, with a view to providing the best ventilation with reasonable durability.
- Use of appropriate items of equipment for hatching and rearing of chicks by broody hens.
- Provision of low-cost appropriate accommodation with security measures for exotic birds of the Model Key Rearers.
- Provision of low-cost lighting facilities for the Model Breeders.
- Choice of low-cost suitable litter materials.
- Determination of the optimum number of day-old chicks to be hatched for best manageable profitability by the Model Mini-Hatchery, by adopting improved appropriate technology devices. Determining the reasons for difficulties that some farmers encounter with this type of enterprise.
- Comparative study of slatted floor and deep litter systems for the Model Breeder unit.
- Conducting of density trials using different breeds or breed combinations to determine the optimum FP flock size.
- Study of the profitability of the broody hen (*desi*) for producing day-old chicks and as caretakers of exotic chicks as foster mothers, and the negative or positive effect on the scavenging behaviour of the chicks.
- Determination of the optimum number of eggs that can be brooded by unit weight or feather density of the *desi* hen, and then the number of chicks that can be successfully reared up to eight weeks of age per *desi* hen, using the creep feeder system of supplementary feeding for growing chicks.
- Study of the effect on the Model Key Rearers' economy if *desi* hens are kept together for brooding purposes.

## Bangladesh model - research in progress

A report on results (completed in mid-2002) from the field-based part of the M.Sc. students' research related to the production and health of rural scavenging poultry in Bangladesh was produced (Permin, 2002) by Danida's Network for Smallholder Poultry Development (NSP) for an INFPD workshop held in Bangladesh in November 2002. Eight post-graduate veterinary and animal production graduates (with field experience in government service in Bangladesh) conducted FP field research (under the Danida and AsDB-assisted PLDP project) towards their M.Sc. (from KVL, Denmark), in the 10-month period from July 2001, in cooperation with the:

- Department of Veterinary Microbiology, The Royal Veterinary and Agricultural University (KVL);
- Department of Animal Science and Health, KVL;

- Danish Institute of Agricultural Sciences;
- Institute for Anthropology, University of Copenhagen;
- Bangladesh Agricultural University;
- Participatory Livestock Development Project in Bangladesh; and
- Danida.

This effort represents the first time that animal scientists and veterinarians have worked together on solving problems directly related to rural poultry production under the difficult logistic conditions in the northwestern districts of Bangladesh covered by PLDP. It is also the first time that problems identified in the field by Danida-supported livestock projects (PLDP and SLDP) in Bangladesh have been fed back to the educational system in Denmark, creating the basis for a new M.Sc. course in rural poultry production and health, supported by a number of research and educational institutions in Denmark and hosted by the Royal Veterinary and Agricultural University in Copenhagen. It is envisaged that the results will be passed on to responsible parties in government and NGOs working on rural development in Bangladesh, thereby enabling an adjustment of the present activities to the ultimate beneficiaries, the poor farmers.

The eight research projects covered a range of important problems relating to scavenging and semi-scavenging poultry production in Bangladesh, notably relating to disease and production aspects. The following list of the eight M.Sc. research project titles is not presented in order of importance, but in connected areas of relevance.

- Helminthosis of free-range chickens in Bangladesh, with emphasis on prevalence and effect on productivity.
- An epidemiological and experimental study of Newcastle Disease in village chickens of Bangladesh.
- Isolation and pathogenic characterizations of Infectious Bursal Disease (IBD) virus isolate from an outbreak of IBD in a rural poultry unit in Bangladesh.
- A longitudinal study of the causes of mortality of chickens in parent stock flocks of the Department of Livestock Services of Bangladesh, with a special emphasis on *Escherichia coli* infection.
- Effect of vitamin A supplementation on vitamin A status, growth parameters and disease resistance of layer type chickens in Bangladesh.
- A study of the effect of feed supplementation on the laying hen under the rural conditions of Bangladesh.
- A study of the effect of feeding systems on the egg production of *Fayoumi* hens of *Model Breeding* units under the PLDP project in Bangladesh.
- A study of the egg production performance of different breeds and breed combinations of chicken in semi-scavenging systems in the PLDP project.

## The Malawi model

Based on a Danida-sponsored study tour to Bangladesh in 2000 (Chinombo *et al.*, 2001), the Malawi Department of Animal Health and Industry learned that the Bangladesh smallholder poultry model is designed as an integrated system to provide the necessary supplies and services to establish an enabling environment for sustainable smallholder FP semi-scavenging production. The FP model consisted of smallholder farmers with small flocks of hens supported by a number of enterprises, all available in the village, to provide inputs and services needed to maintain these flocks. NGO-initiated and motivated farmer groups supported the model. Awareness programmes, training and access to micro-credit was provided to the beneficiaries, the majority of whom were women.

The sustainability of the Bangladesh model relies on a unique implementing organizational structure, involving groups of FP smallholder women farmers, micro-credit, NGOs and government institutions. The study team suggested to their government that the model be replicated in Malawi, with appropriate modification to suit prevailing conditions. For example, Malawi has a much lower population density than Bangladesh and a less developed NGO infrastructure. It was therefore recommended that the Bangladesh model, comprising eight income-generating elements, should be simplified. Results from the Malawi situation analysis (participatory rural appraisal) in the Danida project area showed that the poorest of the poor did indeed exist in the pilot area. By using the criteria of the farmer's perspective, it was found that 37 percent of all households belonged to this poorest segment. It was also found that female-headed households constituted 60 percent of the poorest segment. The analysis further revealed that poultry keeping has a high preference as an income-generating activity, in fact the highest among all livestock categories. The relative status of the importance of different types of livestock was ranked as: sheep, cattle, pigs, goats and chicken.

## The Danida-ENRECA experience in Africa

The abbreviation ENRECA is derived from the Danida objective for the EN-hancement of RE-search CA-pacity in Developing Countries. This is a programme concept of Danida's (Danida-KVL, 2002) in Africa, and involves one poultry project in the United Republic of Tanzania. The immediate aims of the ENRECA programme are to strengthen:

- collaboration on planning and implementation of locally embedded research activities relevant to the national development of the developing countries;
- education at Ph.D. and M.Sc. level;
- the research environment, including such physical facilities as laboratories, libraries and communication facilities; and
- the dissemination of research results to end-users locally as well as internationally.

There are other new FP projects planned for student thesis work in the areas of:

- Newcastle Disease epidemiology in rural poultry production (United Republic of Tanzania);
- disease resistance of rural chicken (United Republic of Tanzania);
- feeding - baseline data and management strategies (Malawi);
- disease interaction - IBD in ducks and chickens (Kenya); and
- *Haemophilus paragallinarum* infection in rural chicken (Uganda).

Initial results from Enreca's Phase 1 (1996-99) in the United Republic of Tanzania are available on the web site <http://www.poultry.kvl.dk/Research/Projects.htm> for the project: "Improving the health and productivity of the rural chicken in Africa", which has formed the basis on which priorities were laid out for a second phase of the project. In terms of collaborative research, the objectives of Phase 2 of the project are to:

- determine optimal and efficient management, feeding and disease control systems under rural conditions, and to implement such systems in selected villages;
- identify and breed the most promising indigenous local chicken Haplotypes (ecotypes), in terms of disease resistance and productivity;
- develop a sustainable Newcastle Disease vaccine campaign under field conditions;
- study and explore the marketing strategy of rural chicken products, to identify and classify the different poultry management systems which exist in the study region and to examine the social, cultural and geographic determinants of these systems; and
- train extension workers and rural farmers in better, but affordable, management, disease control methods and marketing strategies.

Phase 2 of the project is focused on obtaining knowledge of optimal management conditions for FP rural chicken production in Africa. In continuation of this, a Phase 3 will be proposed within three years, to focus on promoting better poultry management practices and disease control, specifically Newcastle Disease control at the village level and on a wider scale (whole districts rather than just a few villages). In addition, and most importantly, Phase 3 will focus on developing village cooperative societies, modelled on the Livestock and Poultry development projects in Bangladesh. In phase 3, models for establishing such cooperatives will be tested in the United Republic of Tanzania, Uganda, Malawi and Kenya, in collaboration with government extension staff and scientists from agricultural, veterinary and social sciences. The farmer cooperatives will have farmers and farmer groups specialized in four production areas:

- producing affordable feeds using locally available feed ingredients;
- raising breeding stock and hatching chicks;
- rearing chicks up to eight weeks of age;
- raising chickens for egg production, sale of eggs and later sale of culls; and /or
- raising chickens for meat under semi-intensive production systems.

## RESEARCH, TRAINING AND EXTENSION NEEDS

The achievement of FP development objectives requires a concerted effort, incorporating research, development and training. A coherent strategy should emphasize, but not be limited to, the following:

- identification of research requirements and programmes, at both the strategic and adaptive levels;
- identification of development efforts for the two target groups: rural and peri-urban;
- delivery of technological assistance to producers with regard to input supply and product marketing; and
- continuous training and retraining of technical staff involved in smallholder FP production at all levels.

In many developing countries, only commercial small-scale intensive (broiler and layer) chicken production is part of the agriculture curriculum in schools. FP chicken production and the production of other poultry species are not considered at any level. For the development of FP production, it is important that this subject be included in the regular education and training schemes of agricultural generalists, as well as livestock and poultry specialists. It is also important that more research on the problems of FP producers be initiated, as this is a precondition for the successful development of FP production. Poultry and livestock specialists in Low Income, Food-Deficient Countries (LIFDCs) must come to accept that the family poultry system is of significant economic and social importance to their countries and is worthy of coordination, examination, intervention and development.

In the past, too much emphasis was given to the development of an autonomous poultry extension system, while the links between poultry production and other agricultural services were neglected. Even if the specialized poultry extension system is well organized and working effectively, its impact on the very large number of smallholder FP keepers (particularly in rural areas) will be very low. This is because government budgets can provide for only a few poultry extension specialists. It is therefore necessary to establish links between poultry specialists and established institutions such as general agricultural extension services, veterinary services, agricultural colleges and NGO services. It is important to revise the strategies and activities of existing poultry farms and stations, so that a considerable part of their capacity is devoted to indirect extension through general extension services.

A study of agricultural training and educational institutions in Africa (FAO, 1984) showed that livestock training facilities were mainly concentrated in North Africa and some West African countries. This means that some African countries do not have the institutional capacity to meet their manpower needs for livestock research, extension and development. It is important that national training institutions be strengthened through utilizing the manpower and training facilities available in other countries. The inauguration of a Regional Poultry Training Programme is an example of such cooperation. The international FP development programme of Danida's Network for Smallholder Poultry Development (NSP) is commendable in its scope, and is committed to the education and training of national scientists and experts in the field. The Fellowships and Networks section later in this chapter presents more details on the NSP foundation, structure, objectives and activities.

## Transfer technology (extension) methodologies

Transfer technology (extension) methodologies (Branckaert *et al.*, 2000) should include a communication strategy for Small livestock Projects for a Food Production (SPFP) framework. A strategy is a systematic process which takes into account the project objectives, the results to be achieved and the technical activities to be carried out. In a participatory planning strategy, it is necessary to identify the needs of the stakeholders and target groups, in order to:

- determine shared values and knowledge and the advantages of the project to be implemented;
- identify the strengths and weaknesses of the topics to be disseminated and identify appropriate tools /media and methodologies;
- assess the constraints (such as limited resources) which are likely to limit the range of alternative actions;
- assess opportunities and threats;
- consider all alternative proposals given to achieve the objectives;
- select the plan which appears to have the greatest chance of achieving the objectives;
- implement the plan and its activities; and
- periodically monitor, evaluate and revise the plan /activities.

A good extension methodology should include a systematic, rational and pragmatic approach to planning, implementing, managing, monitoring, and evaluating effective technology transfer to farmers. An information and extension programme such as the Strategic Extension Campaign (SEC) fits these criteria. FAO's Research, Extension and Training Division (SDR), has recommended this SEC package to AGA for the needs of FP extension. The methodology emphasises the importance of people's participation in strategic planning and systematic management and implementation of information, extension and training programmes. Its training and extension strategies and messages are especially developed from the results of a participatory problem identification process regarding the causes or reasons for non-adoption, or inappropriate practices, of a given recommended technology or innovation.

SEC activities are geared to narrowing the gaps between existing and desired knowledge, attitudes, and appropriate practice levels of the target beneficiaries regarding the technology recommendations. The SEC programme is carried out over a relatively short time period, and aimed at increasing the awareness and knowledge level of target beneficiaries and altering their attitudes and behaviour so as to encourage a favourable adoption of given ideas or sustainable technologies. It follows a systems-approach, which starts with a survey of the target public's Knowledge, Attitude and Practice (a KAP survey), the results of which are used as planning inputs and benchmark baselines for evaluation purposes.

For more detail on how to identify the problems to be faced and overcome in using the SEC (Strategic Extension Campaign) approach, the reader is referred the full text of the paper (Branckaert *et al.*, 2000).

### *Target populations*

The primary target beneficiaries should be the poorest households, women (in particular widows and female-headed households), the disabled (often as a result of civil conflict), women's groups and schools.

## Women

Rural women carry out a fundamental role in agricultural production, rural development and food security. FAO studies and statistics show that women produce between 60 and 80 percent of food in Africa and Asia and approximately 40 percent in Latin America. In many regions, women are also responsible for the management of small livestock, including reproduction. An appropriate approach to working with women and poultry will not only boost productivity and reduce work time, workload and strain, but also promote the transfer of appropriate technology knowledge, tools and skills.

Numerous disparities persist regarding the participation of rural women in poultry production. Undoubtedly they face greater difficulties than men with regard to access to input resources (such as land and credit, among others) and to services designed to increase productivity, for example, research, technology transfer and extension services. Training programmes for women should be planned taking into account their socio-cultural traditions and their high illiteracy rate. In many regions, such programmes should also consider the training of women as extension workers, in order to effectively reach this important target audience.

## Youth

During FAO World Food Day (1999), the theme "Youth against hunger" was given considerable attention, together with the significant role that youth can play in food security. An important message from this event is that given adequate training, education and support, young people can become active partners in helping to meet the World Food Summit goals of halving the number of the hungry by the year 2015.

In terms of technology transfer, many government agricultural extension services include rural youth programming as an integral part of their overall work to help women, men and young farmers apply new practices. An even larger number of NGOs, through extension-type programmes, work to assist youth audiences in the use of improved agricultural technology.

Some of the features of rural youth programmes that make them particularly valuable include their ability to successfully promote the application of technology, such as poultry production, to improve agricultural production on a sustainable basis. Experience has shown that young people are usually more open to new ideas and practices than adult farmers. Most programmes also focus on the start-up of agricultural and rural-based non-agricultural income-generating activities. Any attempt to enhance the knowledge, skills and experience of young people, and increase their access to resources through rural youth programmes, will have an immediate impact on food security.

Rural youth programming, as a technology transfer mechanism, has the potential to overcome some of the major constraints related to expanding FP production in developing countries mentioned earlier in this paper, such as training, management, group organization, disease control, feeding, genetic improvement and protection against predators.

There are already some experiences in developing countries related to the training and education of rural young people in the area of poultry, that, if supported more fully and expanded to other countries, could contribute significantly to more efficient and effective egg and meat production.

Through community-based non-formal educational programming, rural youth gain the necessary knowledge, skills and experiences enabling them to be productive today, as well as to become better farmers for the future. It is essential for farmers to have some knowledge of basic agricultural science related to their daily work. Without this knowledge, the technology often manipulates farmers, often forcing them to act in ways they do not understand, which can be a severe hindrance to effective technology transfer.

Individual and group poultry project activities have been a part of youth programming in some countries for many years. There are two primary ways of reaching young people in rural areas. One is through community-based rural youth programmes, which target out-of-school rural young people. The other is using the rural schools by incorporating agricultural topics as an integral part of the regular curriculum or as extracurricular activities.

Basic poultry science is easily adapted to either community-based groups or school programmes. The most effective way to work with youth in a practical way, either in the community or the schools, is through non-formal education methodology using a hands-on, experiential approach to learning. Community youth members learn such things as basic poultry anatomy and physiology through structured group learning activities and then apply the knowledge to practical experiences, planning and carrying out individual and group small-scale poultry projects.

Where proper facilities are available, small-scale poultry projects can be carried out on the school grounds. Students can learn first-hand many of the practical aspects of raising chickens. The study of embryology by hatching chicken eggs is particularly well suited to the classroom. Much can be learned by students from the incubation and hatching of chicken eggs. Experience around the world has shown that this activity generates much interest and excitement among young people as they anxiously wait 21 days for the eggs to hatch.

One of the constraints to expanded FP production in developing countries is the difficulty of helping farmers organize themselves into groups and associations. This is not a problem where farmers as youth had the experience of being a member of a community or school agricultural club. Belonging to a formal group offers the young person experiences of democratic action with elected officers and structured decision-making. The communication and leadership skills gained enable youth to make immediate contributions to their communities. These skills also help them accept formal and informal leadership roles in community and farmers' organizations as adults.

Through school and community-based rural youth programmes dealing with FP production, youth learn and practice knowledge and skills related to sanitation, vaccination, housing construction using low-cost naturally available materials, predator control, adequate nutrition, improved breeds of chickens and alternative marketing strategies.

As a mechanism for technology transfer, youth programmers, when given adequate support, can make a significant contribution to expanding FP production in developing countries. Young people learn basic principles and sound practices of raising poultry through practical, hands-on projects and activities, enabling them to successfully start and maintain a small enterprise in an efficient and effective manner, thus contributing to food security.

### Disabled - handicapped

During the past decades in many developing countries, civil wars, international conflicts and the dissemination of mines (with their terrible consequences), along with the propagation of handicapping diseases and the increase in traffic accidents, have been responsible for a considerable increase in the number of disabled persons.

For the disabled, FP raising represents a valuable occupation, providing excellent revenue and enabling them to rejoin the social community. Many disabled persons are literate and can thus easily be approached and trained.

### Rural workers

Whatever their gender or age, livestock vaccinators, extension workers and rural development agents need some basic socio-cultural information in order to improve their impact in technology transfer.

The vaccinator needs to know the reasons for the non-adoption of the technology and must be prepared to provide the farmer with a relevant demonstration or explanation. The extension worker should develop extension and training programmes according to the farmer's knowledge and information need. Finally, the development agent should be able to explain the positive advantages for the rural community in having members develop income-generating activities. Specific training programmes and teaching materials, using appropriate media, should be produced to cover these requirements.

## RESEARCH DATA REQUIREMENTS

In anticipation of development assistance under the Special Programme For Food Security (SPFS), FAO provided guidelines for FP field surveys and research (Mack, 1998). Any research or Participatory Rural Appraisal undertaken for FP should ensure that the following list is consulted regarding data collection:

- number of households owning poultry;

- average flock size and breed type;
- flock structure: number of laying hens, cocks, chicks and immature birds;
- average number of eggs laid per clutch and number of clutches per year;
- use of eggs (hatching, sale or home consumption);
- details of any seasonal variation in production or mortality;
- use of male birds and cull hens (sale or consumption);
- selling price (and seasonality) of live birds and eggs at the farmgate and local market;
- estimated income from sale of live birds and eggs;
- estimated production costs (for example, vaccines and feed);
- type of housing provided;
- feeding regime;
- disease control /vaccinations (type and frequency);
- estimates losses (through disease, predators and theft);
- access to goods and services (extension, input supply and marketing);
- perceived constraints; and
- opportunities for expansion.

## Sources of information

Sources for this data could include livestock and agricultural census figures and Veterinary Department records, including:

- vaccination campaigns;
- number of vaccines given;
- supply of locally produced and imported vaccines and their costs; and
- subsidies.

Veterinary Departments should have information on the major epizootic and parasitic diseases that occur in a country, and increasingly there are sections dealing with epidemiology. The Ministry of Agriculture, poultry research institutes and parastatal organizations are sources of information on the technology available, past development experience and the supply of breeding stock, usually from state farms.

Another information source is FAO country production data, which is based on government-submitted information and locally undertaken household surveys or Participatory Rural Appraisals. Other sources include universities, nutrition and home economic departments, the Agricultural Census Office, NGOs and bilateral agencies.

National crop data allows for the use of conversion factors to estimate the supply of agro-industrial by-products and broken grains. Availability is always a concern as these products have many alternative demands, and cost is an important factor. Reports on availability of non-conventional feeds often indicate these alternative uses. Import statistics can give an indication of the level of self-sufficiency for the major animal food products, including eggs and poultry meat. Government household surveys, agricultural census data and local rural appraisal surveys may also provide information on levels of household consumption. If a commercial stock-feed sector exists, they may provide additional information on:

- type of goods (such as feeds, chicks, drugs and vaccines) and services (such as veterinary, public health and abattoirs) that are available and how accessible they are;
- disease situation; and
- supply and demand of feed ingredients.

## DEVELOPMENT CONSIDERATIONS

Many agricultural policy-makers (including livestock specialists) believe that the smallholder poultry system should be considered only as a means of subsistence, and as such needs no coordination, examination, intervention or development. Such notions must be challenged and changed.

Since FAO's first technical assistance project (BGD/79/003) for FP in Bangladesh in 1979, FAO (AGA) has identified, formulated, backstopped and monitored (with the financial assistance of UNDP and the FAO Technical Cooperation Programme [TCP]), many projects supporting FP development activities. The countries involved have included Bangladesh, Burundi, the Democratic Republic of Congo, the Democratic People's Republic of Korea, Ethiopia, the Gambia, Honduras, Maldives, Madagascar, Myanmar, Nigeria, the Philippines, Rwanda, Somalia, the United Republic of Tanzania, Turkey, Viet Nam and Zimbabwe.

The FAO Special Programme for Food Security (SPFS) was launched in 1994 by the FAO Director-General to respond to the urgent need to boost food production. In 1997, improved household poultry production - either peri-urban or rural - was identified as a key element in the overall SPFS approach, and as a major activity of the SPFS diversification component.

The SPFS presently covers 40 countries in Africa, Asia and Latin America. It is rapidly expanding, with more than 60 countries expected to join it during the next few years. The collaboration between SPFS and INFPD will grow simultaneously. The development of South-South cooperation in the field of rural FP is encouraged through the use of Technical Cooperation between Developing Countries (TCDC) experts. Since 1997, important support has also been provided by FAO's Telefood programme. Up to US$10 000/group has been distributed for small-scale FP projects in several countries (Branckaert *et al.*, 2000).

### Productivity objectives

What is required to maximize the productivity of family poultry production systems? First, the whole web of interdependent factors affecting the overall activities of the family farming system, along with their advantages and constraints, must be fully understood. It is certain that village production will continue as long as there are villages, but various aspects of the production system need to be carefully modified. For example, it is now known that vaccination against Newcastle Disease can improve chick survival rate from 30 up to 70 percent; simple housing and other predator protection is required for chicks and young growers; supplementary feeds are important; and other poultry species such as ducks, guinea fowls, pigeons and quails need to be considered.

FP is a vehicle for rural development, income-generation and nutritional enhancement. It is clear that the presence of flourishing industrial peri-urban poultry farms does not negate the need for a parallel FP system in rural areas. Priority must be placed on the development of appropriate technologies, the provision of extension services, farmer training, input and output transportation, markets and credit supply.

It is not appropriate to concentrate entirely on boosting food production at all costs without concern for who produces the food and with what type of management system. FP systems reflect the need to increase job opportunities, stimulate the development of associated non-farming, rural activities and generate benefits that accrue equally to all segments of society, urban as well as rural.

### Fellowships and networks

Development is an ongoing process that requires feedback and constant interaction between operators and the knowledge network, both local and international. The restructuring of the agricultural and livestock extension system towards this approach is an important strategy in poultry development. FAO's Travelling or Visiting Fellowships and regular consultations on poultry development are other examples.

### *INFPD*

The International Network for Family Poultry Development (INFPD), which is supported by FAO, can play a useful role in this regard by promoting:

- exchange and distribution of publications;
- participation in regional and international congresses; and
- the organization of biannual workshops on specialised topics.

The role of the INFPD was expanded from its African focus in 1997, and in December of that year, the first international workshop "Issues in Family Poultry Development Research: Current Concepts in Family Poultry Development Research" was held in M'Bour, Senegal. Proceedings of the workshop (Sonaiya 2000) are also available at:

www.fao.org/ag/aga/AGAP/LPA/fampo1/proceed.htm

### *Danida's Poultry Network*

Danida's "Danish Network for Poultry Production and Health in Developing Countries" was established as a concept in Denmark in 1997 and then renamed the "Network for Smallholder Poultry Development" (NSP) when it became operational in August 1999. The objective of the NSP is "poverty alleviation and improved welfare of the moderate and extreme poor in rural areas". To achieve this, the overall scope of work for the NSP coordination unit is to initiate and coordinate resource bases related to village poultry production in the Danida programme countries (and in Denmark) and to build institutional capacity to implement poultry projects. The coordination unit will promote and carry out research, education and planning of projects, based on experience with the FP smallholder concept in Bangladesh and other countries. This will ensure that necessary education, training, and research will be integrated into the Danida development sector programmes or funded as independent activities. The coordination unit assists in fund-raising for these activities from Danish and international sources. Further information can be found on the website: <http://www.poultry.kvl.dk>

## Socio-economic objectives

To develop effective strategies for family poultry development, some inefficient aspects of traditional production must be replaced by more suitable methods. The main socio-economic objectives of FP development should be to:

- increase rural and peri-urban labour productivity and family incomes through increasing poultry productivity; and
- ensure a high level of food security and raise nutritional levels of rural and peri-urban families.

## Development strategies

The overall aims of development are to reduce poverty and improve income and nutrition. To develop effective strategies for FP development, traditional but inefficient methods of production must be replaced by more suitable measures. The main objectives of such strategies should be:

- improving food supply;
- creating income and employment opportunities for rural populations;
- conserving environmental resources;
- maintaining biodiversity; and
- promoting respect for socio-cultural values.

# Abbreviations and Conversions

| | |
|---|---|
| **AfDB** | African Development Bank |
| **AsDB** | Asian Development Bank |
| **BAU** | Bangladesh Agricultural University, Mymensingh |
| **BCRDV** | Baby Chick Ranikhet Disease Vaccine |
| **BLRI** | Bangladesh Livestock Research Institute, Savar |
| **DLS** | Directorate of Livestock Services |
| **FAO** | Food and Agriculture Organization of the United Nations |
| **GoB** | Government of Bangladesh |
| **GVC** | Government Veterinary College |
| **IBD** | Infectious Bursal Disease (Gumboro disease) |
| **IBDV** | Infectious Bursal Disease Vaccine |
| **IFPRI** | International Food Policy Research Institute |
| **KVL** | The Royal Veterinary and Agricultural University (*Den Kongelige Veterinære Landbohøjskole*) |
| **LIFDC** | Low Income, Food-Deficient Countries |
| **ME** | Metabolisable Energy |
| **ND** | Newcastle Disease (RD: Ranikhet Disease) |
| **NDV** | Newcastle Disease vaccine |
| **NGO** | Non-Governmental Organization |
| **NN** | Naked Neck (Local breed) |
| **NSP** | Network for Smallholder Poultry Development (Danida) |
| **PLDP** | Participatory Livestock Development Project |
| **RIR** | Rhode Island Red (American poultry breed) |
| **SFRB** | Scavengeable Feed Resource Base |
| ***Sonali*** | Bangladeshi poultry breed ("The Golden bird") |
| **SPFP** | Small livestock Projects for Food Production (FAO) |
| **SPFS** | Special Programme for Food Security (FAO) |
| **TCDC** | Technical Cooperation between Developing Countries (FAO) |
| **TCP** | Technical Cooperation Programme (FAO) |
| **Uppazila** | sub district, formerly a *thana* |
| **Velogenic** | highly virulent ND |

## Conversions

### Linear measure

Feet to metres x 0.3048; 3 feet is 0.91 m or 91 cm

### Stock Density

Square feet/bird to Birds/square metre uses an inverse relationship with the multiplier of 0.0929sq.m = 1 sq.ft. Using a calculator, the formula is:

0.0929 M+ then [sq.ft/bird] x, MR, =, /, /, 1, = gives [birds/sq.metre] or

0.0929 M+ then [birds/sq.metre], x, MR, =, /, /, 1, =, gives [sq.ft/bird]

For example: 4.0 sq.ft/bird = 2.7 birds/sq.m

**Energy**

There are 4.1868 megajoules (MJ) or kilojoules (kJ) per megacalorie (Mcal) or kilocalorie (kcal) of energy. The joule is the newer metric format to measure energy.

Example 1: a feed with a metabolisable energy (ME) value of 2300 kcal ME/kg is now stated as 9.6 MJ ME/kg (2300 x 4.1868 / 1000).

Example 2: a SFRB per household of 468 Mcal of ME is now stated as 1960 MJ of ME.

# Bibliography

**Abdou, F.H., Katule, A.M. & Sukuzi, O.S.** 1990. Effect of the pre-incubation storage period of hatching eggs on the hatchability and post-hatching growth of local chickens under tropical conditions. *Beitrage zur Tropischen Landwirtscahft und Veterinarmedizin* 28: 337-342.

**Acharya, R.M. & A. Kumar.** 1984. Performance of local birds in South Asia. *Indian poultry industry yearbook.* 7th Edition.

**Adene, D.F.** 1990. An appraisal of the health management problems of rural poultry stock in Nigeria. *In* E.B. Sonaiya ed. *Rural Poultry in Africa-Proceedings International Workshop held at Ile-Ife, Nigeria:* 89-99.

**Adene, D.F. & Ayandokun, J.O.** 1992. The unfolding order in diseases of poultry in tropical Africa, *Proceedings XIX World Poultry Congress*, Amsterdam, 2: 152-153.

**Adesiyun, A.A., Bishu, G., Adegboye, D.S., & Abdu, P.A.** 1984. Serological survey of Salmonella pullorum antibody in chickens around Zaria, Nigeria. *Bulletin Animal Health and Production in Africa,* 32: 81-85.

**Adeyanju, S.A., Ogutuga, D.B.A., Sonaiya, E.B. & Eshiett, N.** 1978. Evaluation of cocoa husk in finishing diets for broilers. *Turrialba* 27: 371-375.

**Adeyanju, S.A., Ilori J.O. & Osuntogun, C.A.** *Poultry Farming in Ondo State*, undated. Monograph, Ile-Ife, Nigeria. Department of Animal Science, Obafemi Awolowo University. 20 pp.

**Adjovi & Demey**, 1992. Unpublished – reference in Chapter 3 on earthworms for poultry feed.

**Ahmad, A. & Hasnath, M.A.** 1983. *Proceedings SABRAO Workshop on Animal Genetic Resources in Asia and Oceania,* Tropical Agricultural Research Centre, Japan. 418-422.

**Ahmed, N.** 1987. Strategies for livestock disease control for small farmers. *Asian Livestock,*12(10): 110-113.

**Ahmed, N.** 1994. Backyard Poultry feeding systems in Bangladesh. *Asian Livestock XIX,* 7: 73-79.

**Aini, I.** 1990. Indigenous chicken production in south-east Asia. *World Poultry Science Journal,* 46: 125-132

**Akinokun, O.** 1975. The Ife foundation stock of Nigerian chickens: Body weight, egg weight and sexual maturity. *Nigerian Agric. Journal* 12: 232-239.

**Akpapunam, M.A. & Markakis, P.** 1981. Protein supplementation of cowpeas with sesame and watermelon seeds. *J.Food Sci.*, 49: 960.

**Alao, E.A.O. & Sonaiya, E.B.** 1991. *Evaluation of cowpea testa as a protein source for poultry nutrition.* Project report to the Department of Animal Science, Obafemi Awolowo University, Ile-Ife, Nigeria.

**Alam, J.** 1997. Impact of smallholder livestock development project in some selected areas of rural Bangladesh. In *Livestock for Rural Development* (available at www.cipav.org.co/lrrd/lrrd9/bang932.htm).

**Alders, R.G., Inoue, S. & Katongo, J.C.** 1994. Prevalence and evaluation of Hitchner B1 and V4 vaccines for the control of Newcastle disease in village chickens in Zambia. *Prev. Vet. Medicine,* 21(2): 125-132.

**Asuquo, B.O., Okon B.O. & Ekong, A.O.** 1992. Quality parameters of Isa Brown and Nigerian Local Chicken eggs. *Nig. Journal Anim. Prod.,* 19: 1-5.

**Atteh, J.O. & Ologbenla, F.D.** 1993. Replacement of fishmeal with maggots in broiler diets: effects on performance and nutrient retention. *Nig. Journal Anim. Prod.* 20: 44-49.

**Australian Agricultural Consultancy & Management Company (AACMC),** 1984. Livestock subsector Review, 1, Annex.3.

**Ayorinde, K.L.** 1987. Changes in anatomical points of the guinea hens in lay. *Nig. Journal Anim. Prod.* 14: 121-123.

**Ayorinde, K.L., Ayeni, J.S.O. & Okaeme, A.N.** 1984. The production potential of different varieties of the indigenous helmet guinea fowl (*N.m. galeata Pallas*) and the exotic Golden Sovereign (*N.m. meleagris*) in Nigeria. *Proceedings 9th Annual Conference of the Nigerian Society for Animal Production*, Nsukka, Nigeria, 65-72.

**Ba, A.S.** 1982. L´art vétérinaire des pasteurs saheliens. *Fondation pour le Progrès de l´Homme et ENDA,* Dakar: 73-82.

**Baksh, I.** 1994. Permaculture for Poultry. *African Farming,* 1994 (Jan- Feb), 13-14.

**Barua, A., Howlider, M.A.R. & Yoshimura, Y.** 1998. Indigenous Naked Neck fowl of Bangladesh. *World's Poultry Science Journal*, 54, (Sept.1998): 279-286.

**Beker & Banaerjee,** 1990. Cited by Sharnawany and Banerjee, 1991.

**Bell, I.G., Nicholls, P.J., Norman, C., Ideris, A. & Cross, G.M.** 1991. The resistance of meat chickens vaccinated by aerosol with a live V4 Newcastle disease virus vaccine in the field to challenge with velogenic Newcastle disease virus. *Australian Vet. Journal*, 68: 97-101.

**Bell, J.G.** 1990. Strategies for the control of Newcastle disease in village poultry flocks in Africa. *Proceedings International Seminar on Smallholder Rural Poultry Production*, 9-13 October, 1990, Thessaloniki, Greece, 1: 138-143.

**Bell, J.G., Belarbi, D.A. & Amara, A.** 1990a. A controlled vaccination trial for Newcastle disease under village conditions. *Prev. Vet. Medicine*, 9(4): 295-300.

**Bell, J.G., Kane, M. & Le Jan,** C. 1990b. An investigation of the disease status of village poultry in Mauritania. *Prev. Vet. Medicine*, 8(4): 291-294.

**Bessei, W.** 1987. *Tendencies of world poultry production.* Paper presented at the 3rd International DLG-Symposium on Poultry Production in Hot Climates, June 1987, Hameln, Germany.

**Bishop, J.P.**. Undated. Protected Free-Range: *1. Movable Henhouse with Free-Access Range Run for Single-Sire Flock of 25.* Poultry Development Service, Marysville, USA.

**Bishop, J.P.**. Undated. Protected Free-Range: *2. Movable Brooderhouse with Free-Access Range Run for Natural Reproduction of 25 Chicks.* Poultry Development Service, Marysville, USA.

**Bizimana,** N. 1994. Traditional Veterinary Practice in Africa. Deutsche Gessellscahft für Technische Zusammenarbeit (GTZ) GmbH. *Schriftenreihe der GTZ,*No 243, Eschborn.

**Bourzat & Saunders**, 1987. *Improvement of traditional methods of poultry production in Burkina Faso.* Proceedings 3rd International Symposium on Poultry Production in Hot Climates, June, 1987, Hameln, Germany,: 12-15.

**Branckaert, R.D.S.** 1968. Nouvelles données sur l'utilisation des tourteaux de coton en alimentation animale. *Zootechnica* 17(1): 42-50.

**Branckaert, R.D.S. & Guèye, E.F.** 1999. FAO's programme for support to family poultry production. *In* F. Dolberg & P.H. Petersen, eds. *Poultry as a Tool in Poverty Eradication and Promotion of Gender Equality,* 244-256 pp. Proceedings workshop, March 22-26, 1999, Tune Landboskole, Denmark (also available at: http://www.husdyr.kvl.dk/htm/php/tune99/24-Branckaert.htm).

**Branckaert, R.D.S., Gaviria, L., Jallade, J. & Seiders, R.W.** 2000. Transfer of technology in poultry production for developing countries. In *FAO Sustainable Development Dimensions*, October 2000 and *Proceedings WPC2000 Montreal, Canada* (under same title also available at www.fao.org/ag/aga/AGAP/LPA/fampo1/links.htm).

**Burgess, G.W.** 1992. The development of commercial antigen and antibody detection assays for Newcastle disease virus. *In* P.B. Spradbrow, ed. *Proceedings International Workshop Newcastle Disease in Village Chickens: control with thermostable oral vaccines.* 6-10

October, 1992, Kuala Lumpur, Malaysia, *ACIAR Proceedings* ACIAR Monograph No. 39: 25-28.

**Bussi, B**. 1987. *Disease as a constraint on productivity in extensively managed poultry.* University of Edinburgh, Edinburgh. (MSc thesis).

**Chabeuf, N.** 1990. Disease prevention in smallholder village poultry production in Africa. *Proceedings International Seminar on Smallholder Rural Poultry Production,* 9-13 October, 1990. Thessaloniki, Greece (1): 129-138.

**Chavunduka, D.M.** 1976. Plants regarded by Africans as being of medicinal value to animals. *Rhodesian Vet. Journal*, 7(1), 6-12.

**Chen, Bao-Ji.** 1991. Duck production in the Far East and South Pacific. *Poultry International*, 30 (1): 14-18.

**Chinombo, D., Jere, J., Kapelemer-Phiri, G. & Schleiss, K**. (2001). The Malawi smallholder poultry production model (MSPPM): A Poverty reduction strategy. Livestock, Community and Environment. *Proceedings 10th Conference of the Association of Institutions for Tropical Veterinary Medicine*, 2001, Copenhagen, Denmark.

**Chowdhury, S.D., Roy, C.R. & Sarker, A.K.** 1996. Urea in poultry nutrition. *Asian-Australasian Journal Animal Sciences* 9(3): 241-245.

**Coligado, B.C., Lambio A.L. & Luis E.S.** 1986. *U.P.L.B. Res*, 5: 10-13.

**Country Profile,** 1994. Country Profiles or Around the World: Uganda on ducks. *Poultry International,* 33.

**Copland, J. W.** 1987. *Newcastle Disease in Poultry: A New Food Pellet Vaccine.* ACIAR Monograph No. 5: 119.

**Creswell, D.C. & Gunawane, B.** 1982. *Indigenous chickens in Indonesia: production characteristics in an improved environment.* Research Institute for Animal Production, Bogor, Indonesia. Report No. 2: 9-14.

**Dalziel, J.M.** 1937. *The useful plants of West Tropical Africa.* Crown Agents, London, 612 pp.

**Danida-KVL 2002.** *Improving the health and productivity of the rural chicken in Africa* (United Repubilc of Tanzania).Danida-KVL research results 1996-99 Tanzania. *Improving the health and productivity of the rural poultry in Africa* - 2nd phase of an Enreca project (both also available at www.poultry.kvl.dk/IVM_Enreca.htm).

**Danvivatanaporn, J.** 1987. Thailand - Poultry production. *In* J. W. Copland, ed. *Newcastle Disease in Poultry: A New Food Pellet Vaccine.* ACIAR Monograph No. 5: 108-109.

**De Vries, H.** 1995. Performance of free range hybrids in Nicaragua. *ILEIA*,p.28.

**Egbe, O.** 1989. *Utilization of palm oil effluent in layer's diet as an alternative source of energy.* In: G.M.Babatunde, ed. *Proceedings National Workshop Alternative Formulations of Livestock Feeds in Nigeria.* ARMTI, Ilorin. Economic Affairs Office, The Presidency, 723-734.

**Eissa, Y.M.** 1987. Prevalent poultry diseases in hot climate zones and problems of their control. *Zootecnica International,* (Feb): 60-62.

**Elson, H.A.** 1992. *Evaluation of economic aspects of housing systems for layers.* Proceedings XIX World's Poultry Congress, Amsterdam, 2: 503-508.

**Fabiyi, J.P.** 1980. Survey on lice infesting domestic fowl on the Jos Plateau, Northern Nigeria. *Bulletin Animal Health and Production in Africa*, 28: 215-219.

**FAO,** 1961. *Marketing eggs and poultry,* by Stewart and Abbott. FAO Animal Production and Health Series No. 5 and FAO Marketing Guide No. 4. Rome.

**FAO,** 1984. *Rapport de l'Atelier FAO sur le développement de l'aviculture rurale dans les pays francophones de l'Afrique de l'ouest, centrale et de l'est.* Rome.

**FAO,** 1987. *Construction and operation of small solid-wall bins* by O. Bodholt and A. Diop. FAO Agricultural Services Bulletin No. 69. Rome.

**FAO,** 1988. *The role of women in the adoption of new practices.* Paper presented at the World Conference on Animal Production, Helsinki, 1988. 18 pp.

**FAO/UNDP,** 1989. Small Stock Development Project in North Kivu, Zaire. Monograph, Rome.

**Farina, L., Demey, F. & Hardouin, J.** 1991. Production de termites pour l'aviculture villageoise au Togo. *Tropicultura* ,9 (4): 181-187.

**Farrell, D.J**. 1986. Energy expenditure of laying ducks: confined and herded. *In* D.J. Farrell and P. Stapleton, eds. *Duck Production Science and World Practice*, 70-82. University of New England, Armidale, NSW.

**Farrell, D.J.** 1997. Integrated wetland rice and duck production systems in humid tropics of Asia: Current and future trends. *Proceedings 11$^{th}$ European Symposium on Waterfowl*, Nantes (France), 483-489.

**Fatihu, M.Y., Ogbogun, V.C., Njoku, C.O., & Saror, D.I.** 1992. Observations on lesions associated with some gastrointestinal nematodes of chickens in Zaria, Nigeria. *Bulletin Animal Health and Production in Africa*, 40(1), 15-18.

**Fattah, K.A.,** 1999. Poultry as a tool in poverty eradication and promotion of gender equality. *In* F. Dolberg and P.H. Petersen, eds. *Poultry as a Tool in Poverty Eradication and Promotion of Gender Equality,* pp.16-28. Proceedings workshop, March 16-22 1999, Tune Landboskole, Denmark (also available at http://www.husdyr.kvl.dk/htm/php/tune99/2-Fattah.htm).

**Forssido, T**. 1986. *Studies on the meat production potential of some local strains of chickens in Ethiopia.* Justus-Liebig University, Giessen, Germany. (PhD thesis).

**French, K.M**. 1981. *Practical Poultry Raisings*. Peace Corps Information Collection and Exchange, pp.153-168. Washington, DC.

**Fuan, Liu 1987.** The parched rice incubation technique for hatching duck eggs. *In* D.J.Farrell and P. Stapleton, eds. *Duck Production Science and World Practice*, pp.178-182. University of New England, Armidale, NSW.

**Gaffar Elamin, M.A., Khalafalla, A.I., & Ahmed, S.M.** 1993. Observations on the use of Komarov strain of Newcastle disease vaccine in the Sudan. *Tropical Animal Health and Production*, 25: 151-154.

**George, J.B.D., Otobo, S., Ogunleye, J., & Adediminiyi, B.** 1993. Louse and mite infestation in domestic animals in northern Nigeria. *Tropical Animal Health and Production*, 25, 121-124.

**Gunaratne, S.P., Chandrasiri, A.D.N., Hemalatha, W.A.P.M., & Roberts, J.A.** 1993. Feed resource base for scavenging village chickens in Sri Lanka. *Tropical Animal Health and Production* 26: 249-257.

**Gunaratne, S.P, Chandrasiri, A.D.N., Wickramaratne, S.H.G. & Roberts, J.A.** 1994. The utilisation of scavenging feed resource base for village chicken production. *Proceedings Seventh Asian Australasian Association for Animal Production Congress*, Bali, Indonesia, 2: 67-68.

**Guéye, E.F.** 1998. Village egg and fowl meat production in Africa. *World's Poultry Science Journal* 54 (1): 73-86.

**Haaren-Kiso, A., Horst, van, P. & Valle Zarate, A.** 1995. Direct and indirect effects of the frizzle gene on the productive adaptability of laying hens. *Animal Research and Development*, 42: 98-114.

**Hahn, D.T., Hai L.T., Hung D.S., & Tinh, N.H.** 1995. Improving the productivity of local Muscovy duck with high yielding exotic Muscovy duck and the initial production experiment of Mullard in Vietnam. *Proceedings 10$^{th}$ European Symposium on Waterfowl*, Halle, Germany. World's Poultry Science Association, 31-39.

**Huque, Q.M.E.** 1999. Poultry research in Bangladesh: present status and its implication for future research. *In* F. Dolberg and P.H. Petersen, eds. *Poultry as a Tool in Poverty*

*Eradication and Promotion of Gender Equality,* pp.151-164. Proceedings workshop, March 22-26, 1999, Tune Landboskole, Denmark (also available at http://www.husdyr.kvl.dk/htm/php/tune99/15-Haque.htm).

**Horst, P.** 1989. Native fowl as reservoir for genomes and major genes with direct and indirect effect on adaptability and their potential for tropical orientated breeding plans. *Arch. Geflügelkd.* 53: 93-101.

**Horst, P.** 1990a. Waterfowl in China. *Poultry International* , 29(4): 16-20.

**Horst, P**. 1990b. Research and development perspectives. *Proceedings International Seminar on Smallholder Rural Poultry Production*, 9-13 October, 1990, Thessaloniki, Greece, pp. 61-69.

**Huchzermeyer, F.W.** 1973. Free-ranging hybrid chickens under African tribal conditions. *Rhodesian Agricultural Journal*, 70: 73-75.

**Horst, P., Mathur P.K. & Valle Zarate, A.** 1996. Breeding policies for specific tropical environments using appropriate combinations of major genes. *Proceedings XX World Poultry Congress*, New Delhi, India, 1: 633-640.

**Hutagalung, R.I.** 1981. The use of tree crops and their by-products for intensive animal production. *In* A.J.Smith and R.G. Gunn, eds. *Intensive animal production in the developing countries,*. Occasional Publication No. 4. British Society of Animal Production. 151-184 pp.

**Ideris, A., Ibrahim, A. L., & Spradbrow, P. B.** 1990. Vaccination of chickens against Newcastle disease with a food pellet vaccine. *Avian Pathology*, 19(2): 371-384.

**Jagne, J., Aini, I., Schat, K. A., Fennell, A., & Touray, O.** 1991. Vaccination of village chickens in the Gambia against Newcastle disease using the heat-resistant, food-pelleted V4 vaccine. *Avian Pathology*, 20(4), 721-724.

**Janviriyasopak, O., Thitisak, W., Thepkraiwan, L., Jongsathien, K., Mekapratheep, M., von Kruedner, R. & Morris, R.S.** 1989. *A health and productivity study of village poultry.* Proceedings of the International Seminar on Animal Health and Production Services for Village Livestock. Khon Kaen Thailand. 161-171.

**Jayawardane, G.W.L., Alwis, M.C.L.D., & Bandara, D.A.W.W.D.A.** 1990. Oral vaccination of chickens against Newcastle disease with V4 vaccine delivered on processed rice grains. *Australian Veterinary Journal*, 67(10): 364-366.

**Jensen, H.A.,** 1999 Paradigm and Visions: Network for Poultry Production and Health in Developing Countries. *In* F. Dolberg and P.H. Petersen, eds. *Poultry as a Tool in Poverty Eradication and Promotion of Gender Equality,* pp.31-38. Proceedings workshop, March 22-26, 1999, Tune Landboskole, Denmark (also available at http://www.husdyr.kvl.dk/htm/php/tune99/3-AJensen.htm).

**Kabatange, M.A. & Katule, A.M.** 1989. Rural poultry production systems in the United Republic of Tanzania. *In* E. B. Sonaiya, ed. *Rural poultry in Africa.* Proceedings of an International Workshop, Ile-Ife, Nigeria, 13-16 November, 1989: 171-176.

**Katule, A.M.** 1991. Performance of local chickens under scavenging and intensive management systems. *Entwicklung ländlicher raum* 5: 26-28.

**Kelly, P. J., Chitauro, D., Rohde, C., Rukwava, J., Majok, A., Davelaar, F., & Mason, P. R.** 1994. Diseases and management of backyard chicken flocks in Chitungwiza, Zimbabwe. *Avian Diseases*, 38(3): 626-629.

**Khadijah, E.** 1988. University Malaya, Kuala Lumpur 212. (PhD thesis).

**Khalafalla, A..I.** 1994. Isolation and characterization of lentogenic Newcastle disease viruses from apparently healthy chickens in the Sudan. *Bulletin Animal Health and Production in Africa*, 42(3): 179-182.

**Khomari, L.** 2000 (Chairperson) Final Discussion: Lessons for Future Research and Development: how do we use data to develop a rural poultry development programme? *In*

E.B. Sonaiya, ed. *Issues in Family Poultry Development Research.* 2000. Proceedings International workshop on December 9-13, 1997, M'Bour, Senegal. INFPD, Department of Animal Science, Faculty of Agriculture, Obafemi Awolowo University, Ile-Ife, Nigeria (also available at http://www.fao.org/ag/aga/AGAP/LPA/fampol/proceed.htm).

**Kim, S.J., & Spradbrow, P.B**. 1978. Some properties of lentogenic Australian Newcastle disease virus. *Veterinary Microbiology*, 3: 129-141.

**Kingston, D.J.** 1980. The productivity of scavenging chickens in some villages of West Java, Indonesia. *Proceedings of the South Pacific Poultry Science Convention,* Auckland, New Zealand. 228-236.

**Kingston, D.J & Creswell, D.C** 1982. *Indigenous chickens in Indonesia: population and production characteristics in five villages in West Java.* Research Institute for Animal Production, Bogor, Indonesia, Report No. 2, 3-8.

**Kobling, S.** 1989. Abschlußbericht, Station Avicole Dosso, Niger. GTZ. 8 pp.

**Koeslag, G.J**. 1992. The role of poultry in the rural areas. *Proceedings of the Introductory Seminar on Poultry Development Policy*, 7-16 September 1992, Barneveld College, Barneveld, The Netherlands. 17-23.

**Koster, E. (Ed.)** 1996. Poultry Farming Systems for Small Commercial Farmers. *Proceedings of a Poultry Workshop held at the Animal Improvement Institute*, Irene, South Africa.

**Mack, S.** 1998. Type and sources of information on family poultry. *INFPD Newsletter* 8 (2) February - March 1998. From *Guidelines for the inclusion of improved household poultry production, Special programme for food security (SPFS*), May, 1997:13-14. AGA Divisional SPFS Focal Point, FAO, Rome.

**Majiyagbe, K.A. & Nawathe, D.R.** 1981. Isolation of virulent Newcastle disease virus from apparently normal ducks in *Nigeria. Vet. Record*, 108(9): 190.

**Mathur, P.K. & Horst, P.** 1989. Temperature stress and tropical locations as factors for genotype x environment interactions in poultry production. *Proceedings Genotype and environment interactions in poultry production*, INRA, Jouy-en-Josas (France): 83-96.

**Matthewman, R.W**. 1977. *A survey of Small Livestock at the village level in derived Savanna and Lowland Forest Zones of South West Nigeria.* Study No. 4, University of Reading.

**Mavale, A.P**. 1995. *Epidemiology and control of Newcastle disease in rural poultry in Mozambique.* University of Reading, Reading. (MSc thesis).

**Mbugua P.N.** 1990. *Proceedings Rural Small-holder Poultry Production in Kenya,* 2: 119-131.

**McInerney, J**. 1992. Economic aspects of disease in poultry production. *Proceedings XIX World Poultry Congress*, 2: 561-566.

**Meulemans, G., Letellier, C., Gonze, M., Carlier, M.C., & Burny, A.** Recombinant vaccinia virsu vector protects chickens against live-virus 1988. Newcastle disease virus F glycoprotein expressed from a challenge. *Avian Pathology*, 17: 821-827.

**Mkangare, M.M.J.** 1989. *Collection of Tanzanian medicinal plants for biological activity studies.* Paper presented at the 7th Tanzanian Veterinary Association, Dar-es-Salaam, United Republic of Tanzania.

**Moerad, B.** 1987. Indonesia: Disease Control. *In* J. W. Copland, ed. *Newcastle Disease in Poultry: A New Food Pellet Vaccine.* ACIAR Monograph No. 5: 73-76.

**National Research Council** 1984. *Nutrient Requirements of Poultry*. Subcommittee on Poultry Nutrition, National Academy Press, Washington, DC.

**Nawathe, D. R.** 1982. Isolation of poxvirus from an outbreak in turkey poults. *Sudan Journal of Veterinary Science and Animal Husbandry*, 23(2), 140-141.

**Negesse, T**. 1991. Survey of internal parasites of local chickens of southern Ethiopia. *Indian Journal of Poultry Science*, 26(2): 128-129.

**Nielsen, H.** 2000. *Food and nutrient intake among females in rural Bangladesh - how does a poultry project benefit women and girls?* Research Department of Human Nutrition. The Royal Veterinary and Agricultural University. Copenhagen. (MA thesis).

**Nwokolo, E.N., Bragg, D.B. & Saben, H.S.** 1977. A nutritive evaluation of palm kernel meal for use in poultry rations. *Tropical Science* 19: 147-154.

**Nwosu, C.C.** 1979. Characterization of the local chicken of Nigeria and its potential for egg and meat production. *Proceedings 1st national Seminar on Poultry Production in Nigeria*, 11-13 December, Ahmadu Bello University, Zaria, Nigeria. National Animal Production Research Institute, 187-210.

**Nwude, N. & Ibrahim, M.A.** 1980. Plants used in traditional veterinary medical practice in Nigeria. *J. Vet. Pharmacol. & Therapeutics*, 3: 261-273.

**Obi, O.O. & E.B. Sonaiya.** 1995. Gross margin analysis of smallholder rural poultry production in Osun State. *Nig. Journal Anim. Prod.*, 22: 95-107.

**Odi, H. Diambra.** 1990. State of smallholder rural poultry production in Cote d'Ivoire. *Proceedings International Seminar on Smallholder Rural Poultry Production,* 9-13 October, 1990, Thessaloniki, Greece, pp.105-116.

**Oh, B.T**. 1987. Malaysia: Economic importance. *In* J.W.Copland, ed. *Newcastle Disease in Poultry - A New Food Pellet Vaccine*, ACIAR Monograph No. 5: 83-85.

**Ojeniyi, A.** 1984. *Salmonella hirschfeldi* in poultry and humans in Ibadan, Nigeria. *Bulletin of the World Health Organization*, 62(5), 773-775.

**Ojeniyi, A. A.** 1985. Comparative bacterial drug resistance in modern battery and free-range poultry in a tropical environment. *Vet. Record*, 117(1), 11-12.

**Olawoye, J.E. & D.C. di Domenico**, 1990. *Socio-cultural factors related to livestock production in southern Nigeria.* Paper presented at the National conference on Nigerian livestock industry and prospects for the 1990s, 19-22, November, 1990, Kaduna, Nigeria. NISER, 18 pp.

**Olori, V. E. & E. B. Sonaiya.** 1992a. Composition and shell quality of white and brown eggs of the Nigeria Indigenous chicken. *Nig. Journal Anim. Prod.*, 19:12-14.

**Olori, V. E. & E. B. Sonaiya.** 1992b. Effect of length of lay of Nigeria Indigenous chickens on their egg composition and shell quality. *Nig. Journal Anim. Prod.* 19:95-100.

**Oluyemi, J.A.** 1979. *Potentials of the indigenous species of poultry for meat and egg production in Nigeria.* pp.163-186. Proceedings 1st National Seminar on Poultry Production in Nigeria, 11-13 December, 1979. Ahmadu Bello University, Zaria, Nigeria. National Animal Production Research Institute.

**Oluyemi, J.A. & Roberts F.A.** 1988. *Manure parameters: poultry production in warm wet climates*, p.113. London, Macmillan.

**Omeje, S.S.I. & Nwosu, C.C.** 1986. *3rd World Congress: Genet. Appl. Livest. Prod.*, Nebraska. X: 304-310.

**Onwudike, O.C.** 1986. Palm kernel as a feed for poultry. *Animal Feed Science and Technology* 16: 179-202.

**Ouandaogo, Z.C.** 1990. Programme de développement des animaux villageois (PDAV), *Proceedings International Seminar on Smallholder Rural Poultry Production,* 9-13 October, 1990, Thessaloniki, Greece, (2): 27-36.

**Prasetyo, T., Subiharta, W.D., & Sabrani, M.** 1985. *The effect of chick and hen separation on village chicken egg productivity.* 1984/1985 Research Report, p.22. Research Institute for Animal Production, Indonesia.

**Prawirokusumo, S.** 1988. Problems to improve small scale native chickens management in south-east asian countries. *Proceedings XVIII World's Poultry Congress*, Japan, 113-116.

**Ramm G., Balzer, G., Eckert, M. v., Hugo, R., Massler, B., Müller, R., & Richter, J.** 1984. *Animal Husbandry in East Kalimantan: integration of animal husbandry into transmigrant* *farming systems in the middle Mahakam area in East Kalimantan, Indonesia.*Fachbereich Internationale Agraentwicklung, Technische Universität Berlin, Berlin, Publication No.84, 4-5.

**Ratanasethakul, C**. 1988. Study of Newcastle disease vaccination one to four times a year in native chickens raised in the village. *Thai Journal of Vet. Medicine,* 18(1): 3-7.

**Rauen, H.W, de los Santos, M. & Fabian, P.** 1990. Actual situation of the small scale poultry production in rural areas in the Dominican Republic and improving perspectives for the future. *Proceedings International Seminar on Smallholder Rural Poultry Production*, 9-13 October, 1990, Thessaloniki, Greece,.

**Roberts, J.A.**, 1999. Utilisation of Poultry Feed Resources by Smallholders in the Villages of Developing Countries. *In* F. Dolberg & P.H. Petersen, eds. *Poultry as a Tool in Poverty Eradication and Promotion of Gender Equality,* pp. 311-336. Proceedings workshop, March 22-26, 1999, Tune Landboskole, Denmark.
(available at http://www.husdyr.kvl.dk/htm/php/tune99/28-roberts.htm).

**Roberts, J.A., Gunaratne, S.P., Wickramaratne, S.H.G & Chandrasiri, A.D.N.** 1994. *Proceedings of the Seventh Asian-Australasian Association for Animal Production Congress*, Bali, Indonesia, 2: 34-35.

**Roberts, J.A. & Senaratne, R.** 1992. The successful introduction of hybrid egg laying chickens into a Sri Lankan village. *Proceedings 19th World Poultry Congress*, Amsterdam, 1: 818-821.

**Sa'idu, L., Abdu, P.A., Umoh, J.U. & Abdullahi, U.S.** 1994. Diseases of Nigerian indigenous chickens. *Bulletin Animal Health and Production in Africa,* 42(1): 19-23.

**Sagild, I.K. & Haresnape, J.M.** 1987. The status of Newcastle disease and the use of V4 vaccine in Malawi. *Avian Pathology*, 16(1): 165-176.

**Sagild, I.K. & Spalatin, J.** 1982. Newcastle disease vaccination with the V4 strain in Malawi. Laboratory and field studies. *Avian Diseases*, 26: 625.

**Salatin, J. 1993**. *Pastured Poultry Profits*. Swoope, Virginia, Polyface Inc.

**Saleque, M.A.** 1999. Scaling-up: Critical factors in leadership, management, human resource development and institution-building in going from pilot project to large-scale implementation: The BRAC poultry model in Bangladesh. *In* F. Dolberg & P.H. Petersen, eds. *Poultry as a Tool in Poverty Eradication and Promotion of Gender Equality,* pp. 51-71. Proceedings workshop, March 22-26, 1999, Tune Landboskole, Denmark (also available at http://www.husdyr.kvl.dk/htm/php/tune99/5-Saleque.htm).

**Sall, B.** 1990. *Contribution a l'etude des possibilites d'amelioration de la production en aviculture traditionnelle: mesure du potentiel de la race locale et des produits d'un croisement ameliorateur.* Institut National de Developpement Rural, St. Louis, Senegal. P. 32 (MSc thesis).

**Samson, A.C.R.** 1988. Virus structure. *In:* D. J. Alexander, ed. *Newcastle Disease*, pp. 23-44. Kluger Academic Publishers, London.

**Samuel, J.L., Bensink, Z., & Spradbrow, P.B**. 1993. Oral vaccination of chickens with the V4 strain of Newcastle disease virus: Cooked and raw white rice as a vehicle. *Tropical Animal Health and Production*, 25: 3-10.

**Samuel, J.L. & Spradbrow, P.B**. 1989. Persistence of the V4 strain of Newcastle disease virus in open-range flock of chickens. *Vet. Records*, 124: 193-196.

**Sani, R.A., Harisah, M., Ideris, A. & Shah-Majid, M.** 1987. Malaysia: Fowl diseases. *In:* J. W. Copland, ed. *Newcastle disease in poultry: a new food pellet vaccine.* ACIAR Monograph No. 5: 89-92.

**Saunders, M.J.** 1984. *La trichose de la pintade en Haute-Volta: une protozoose meutriere et meconnue.* Projet de Développement de l'Aviculture Villageoise, Ministère du Développement Rural, Ouagadougou, Burkina Faso.

**Sazzad, M.H, Ebadul, M.H. & Asaduzzaman, M.U.** 1990. Egg production by desi (indigenous) hens in rural Bangladesh. *Tropical Animal Health and Production* 22:22.

**Setioko, A.R.** 1997 Recent study on traditional system of duck layer flock management in Indonesia. *Proceedings 11th European Symposium on Waterfowl,* 8-10 September, 1997, Nantes (France), 491-498.

**Sharma, R.N., Hussein, N.A., Pandey, G.S. & Shandomo, M.N.** 1984 A study on Newcastle disease outbreaks in Zambia, 1975-1984. *Revue Scientifique et Technique,* Office International des Epizooties, 5(1): 5-14.

**Shingari, B.K., Sapra, K.L. & Mehta, R.K.** 1994. Guinea fowl in the Punjab. *Poultry International,* 33(7): 54.

**Siddiqui, S., Tarik, N., Bina, S.S. & Shaheen, F.** 1986. Isolation of a triterpenoid from Azadirachta indica. *Phytochemistry* 25(9): 2183-2186.

**Simmons, G.C.** 1967. The isolation of Newcastle disease in Queensland. *Australian Veterinary Journal,* 43: 29.

**Smith, A.J.** 1990. *Poultry-Tropical Agriculturist Series,* pp.179-184.CTA, Macmillan, London.

**Smith, O.B., Ilori, J.O. & Onesirosan, P.** 1984. The proximate composition and nutritive value of the winged bean *Phosphocarpus tetragonolobus* (L) DC for broilers. *Animal Feed Science & Tech.* 11: 231-237.

**Sonaiya, E.B.** 1989. Animal by-products and their potential for commercial livestock feed production. *In*: G.M. Babatunde, ed. *Proceedings National Workshop on Alternative Formulations of Livestock Feeds in Nigeria.* ARMTI, 21-15 November, 1988, Ilorin, Nigeria, Economic Affairs Office, The Presidency, 298-315.

**Sonaiya, E.B.** 1990a. The context and prospects for development of smallholder rural poultry production in Africa. *Proceedings International Seminar on Smallholder Rural Poultry Production,* 9-13 October, 1990, Thessaloniki, Greece, 1: 35-52.

**Sonaiya, E.B.** 1990b, ANRPD Proceedings International Network for Family Poultry Development (INFPD): origins, activities, objectives and visions. *In* F. Dolberg & P.H. Petersen, eds. *Poultry as a Tool in Poverty Eradication and Promotion of Gender Equality,* pp.39-50. Proceedings Workshop, March 22-26, 1999, Tune Landboskole, Denmar (also available at http://www.husdyr.kvl.dk/htm/php/tune99/4-Sonaiya.htm).

**Sonaiya, E.B**. 1990c. Poultry husbandry in small rural farms.*Entwicklung + ländlicher raum* 4: 3-6.

**Sonaiya, E.B.** 1992. *The Guinea fowl: the status of knowledge in the arid to the sub-humid zones of West Africa.* Paper presented to the FAO workshop on Guinea fowl Development in African Dry Areas, Ouagadougou, Burkina Faso. October 18-24, 1992

**Sonaiya, E.B.** 1993. Evaluation of non-conventional feed ingredients as supplements for scavenging chicken. *Proceedings VII World Conference on Animal Production,* 1993, Edmonton, Alberta, 28-29.

**Sonaiya, E.B**. 1995. Feed resources for smallholder poultry in Nigeria. *World Animal Review,* 82 (1): 25-33.

**Sonaiya, E.B.** 2000. *Issues in Family Poultry Development Research.* Proceedings International workshop Dec. 9-13, 1997 at M'Bour, Senegal. INFPD, pp. 204. Ile-Ife, Nigeria, Dept. Animal Science, Faculty of Agriculture, Obafemi Awolowo University. (Also available at http://www.fao.org/ag/aga/AGAP/LPA/fampo1/fampo.htm).

**Sonaiya, E.B. Branckaert, R.D.S. & Guèye, E.F.** 1999. *Research and development options for family poultry.* Introductory paper to the First INFPD/FAO electronic conference on family poultry, December 1998 to July 1999 (also available at http://www.fao.org/ag/aga/AGAP/LPA/fampo1/fampo/Intropap.htm).

**Sonaiya, E.B. & Omole, T.A.** 1977. Cassava peels for finishing pigs. *Nutrition Reports International* 16(4): 479-486.

**Soukossi, A.** 1992. Maggot production for fish and poultry production. *ANRPD Newsletter* 3(2): 6.

**Spradbrow, P.B.** 1993/94. Newcastle disease in village chickens. *Poultry Science Review*, 5(2): 57-96.

**Ssenyonga, G. S.** 1982. Prevalence of helminth parasites of domestic fowl (*Gallus domesticus*) in Uganda. *Tropical Animal Health and Production* 14:201-204.

**Sugrim, A.M.** 1987. Role of livestock in socio-economic development of small farmers in the Pacific Island countries. *Asian Livestock* (October 1987): 127-131.

**Suleiman, H.** 1990. An address to the International workshop on Rural Poultry Development. *In:* E. B. Sonaiya, ed. *Rural Poultry in Africa.* Proceedings International Workshop, 13-16 November, 1989, Ile-Ife, Nigeria, African Network on Rural Poultry Development (ANRPD), 7-8.

**Supramaniam, P.** 1988. Economic importance of Newcastle disease vaccine to the village poultry industry in Malaysia. *Proceedings Second Asian/Pacific Poultry Health Conference*, 13-25 September, 1988, Surfers' Paradise, Australia,: 511-516.

**Tadelle, D., Alemu, Y. & Peters, K.J.** 2000. Indigenous chickens in Ethiopia: genetic potential and attempts at improvement. *World Poultry Science Journal*, 56(1): 45- 54.

**Tantaswasdi, U., Danvivatanaporn, J., Siriwan, P., Chaisingh, A. & Spradbrow, P.B.** 1992. Evaluation of an oral Newcastle disease vaccine in Thailand. *Prev. Vet. Medicine*, 12, 87-.

**ter Horst, K.** 1986. *Poultry Management in rural areas of developing countries: Matching technical demands with social facts.* Unpublished report, Department of Livestock Services, Ministry of Livestock and Fisheries, Bangladesh.

**ter Horst, K.** 1987 *Some remarks on poultry improvement in Bangladesh as related to socio-economic factors.* Paper presented to the FAO Expert Consultation on Rural Poultry Development in Asia, Dhaka, Bangladesh.

**The Bin, N.** 1996. Economic efficiency of duck raising in the Mekong River Delta, *In* W.J. Pryor, ed. *ACIAR Proceedings*, ACIAR Monograph No. 68: 138-145.

**Thitisak, W.** 1992. *Untersuchungen über die Häufigkeit und Ursachen der Abgänge bei der kleinbäuerlichen Geflügelhaltung in Nordosten Thailands.* Unpublished Dr Med. Vet., Tierärtzlichen Hochschule Hannover, Hannover. 84p.

**Thitisak, W., Janviriyasopak, O., Morris, R.S., Srihakim, S. & Kruedener, R. V.** 1989. Causes of death found in an epidemiological study of native chickens in Thai villages. *Acta Veterinaria Scandinavia,* 84 (Suppl.): 200-202.

**Tucker, S.** 1989. Alternatives, *ADAS Poultry Journal* 3(1): 15-30.

**Udedibie, A.B.I.** 1991. Relative effects of heat and urea-treated jackbean (*Canavalia ensiformis*) and swordbean (*Canavalia gladiata*) on the performance of laying hens. *Livestock Research for Rural Development*, 3(3): 68-76.

**Udo, H.** 1992. Are free range poultry relevant? *N-CT-R Livestock Newsletter* 5(2): 2.

**van Veluw, K.** 1987. Traditional poultry keeping in Northern Ghana. *ILEIA,* December 1987, 3(4): 12-13.

**Verger, M.** 1986. La prophylaxie de la maladie de Newcastle dans les élevages villageois en Afrique. *L'aviculteur*, 465: 44-48.

**Vorster, A., Adjovi, A., Demey, F.** 1992. Protéines dans les aliments des poules–l'utilisation d'Eudrilus eugeniae et Eisenia fetida dans des conditions tropicales. *Bulletin du RADAR.*,2(1):3.

**Watt, J.M. & Breyer-Brandwijk, M.G.** 1962. *The Medicinal and Poisonous Plants of Southern and Eastern Africa.* E & S Livingstone Ltd, Edinburgh and London.

**Wibberley, G.** 1994. Monitoring of highly virulent infectious bursal disease in Botswana 1989 to 1993. *Tropical Animal Health and Production,* 26(3): 161-162.

**Wickramaratne, S.H.G., Gunaratne, S.P., Chandrasiri, A.D.N. & Roberts, J.A.** 1994. Chick mortality in scavenging village chickens in Sri Lanka. *Proceedings of the Asian-Australasian Association for the Advancement of Animal Production,* Bali, Indonesia, 2: 71-72.

**Young, J.R.** 1987. Training of Community Animal First Aid Workers. *ILEIA,* December, 3(4): 14-15.

**Young, P**. 1991. The use of heat resistant V4 Newcastle disease vaccine in Asia. *In*: F. Demey & V. S. Pandey, eds. *Newcastle disease vaccination of village poultry in Africa and Asia.* Proceedings seminar, Antwerp, Belgium, Feb.13-14, 1991, 19-27.

**Zoungrana, B. & Slenders, G.,** 1993. Poultry in the Backyard in Burkina Faso. *ILEIA*, 18(3): 17.

**Wickramaratne, S.H.G., Gunaratne, S.P., Chandrasiri, A.D.N. & Roberts, J.A.** 1994. Chick mortality in scavenging village chickens in Sri Lanka. *Proceedings of the Asian-Australasian Association for the Advancement of Animal Production*, Bali, Indonesia, 2: 71-72.

**Young, J.R.** 1987. Training of Community Animal First Aid Workers. *RERA* December, 3(4): 14-15.

**Young, P.** 1991. The use of heat resistant V4 Newcastle disease vaccine in Asia. In: **J. Demey & V. S. Pandey**, eds. *Newcastle disease vaccination of village poultry in Africa and Asia*. Proceedings seminar, Antwerp, Belgium, Feb. 13-14, 1991, 19-27.

**Zoungrana, B. & Slenders, G.** 1992. Poultry in the Backyard in Burkina Faso. *ILEIA*, 18(3): 17.